THE
TRANSATLANTIC
SLAVE TRADE

THE
TRANSATLANTIC
SLAVE TRADE

Overcoming the 500-Year Legacy

DR. BENJAMIN F. CHAVIS, JR.
STACY M. BROWN

SelectBooks, Inc.
New York

This edition published by SelectBooks, Inc.
For information address SelectBooks, Inc., New York, New York.

First Edition

ISBN 978-1-59079-569-9

Library of Congress Cataloging-in-Publication Data

Names: Chavis, Ben, 1948- author. | Brown, Stacy, 1968- author.
Title: The transatlantic slave trade : overcoming our 500-year legacy /
Benjamin F. Chavis Jr., Stacy M. Brown.
Description: New York : SelectBooks, [2024] | Includes bibliographical
references and index. | Summary: "Authors affirm that the Transatlantic
Slave Trade was the longest-running genocidal crime against humanity in
world history, causing the death, enslavement, and suffering of
approximately 25 million African people for centuries in the Western
Hemisphere, and support the United Nation's Report citing concrete steps
to address the continued harm suffered by people of African descent"--
Provided by publisher.
Identifiers: LCCN 2024011312 (print) | LCCN 2024011313 (ebook) | ISBN
9781590795699 (hardcover) | ISBN 9781590795705 (ebook) |
Subjects: LCSH: Transatlantic slave trade. | Slavery--History. | Enslaved
persons--History. | African diaspora. | Black people--Social conditions.
Classification: LCC HT1331 .C43 2024 (print) | LCC HT1331 (ebook) | DDC
306.3/62091821--dc23/eng/20240606
LC record available at https://lccn.loc.gov/2024011312
LC ebook record available at https://lccn.loc.gov/2024011313

Manufactured in the United States of America
10 9 8 7 6 5 4 3 2 1

CONTENTS

Foreword

by Chuck D

*T*he transatlantic slave trade is a brutal scar on the face of humanity, a monstrous crime that tore millions of Africans from their homeland, dehumanized them, and built the so-called American dream on their blood, sweat, and tears. This isn't just history—it's the very foundation of the systemic racism that still plagues America today. If you want to understand the real roots of our struggle, you've got to go back to where it all began. And that's exactly what this book does—unflinchingly and unapologetically.

The journey of enslaved Africans across the Atlantic was a journey into hell. Crammed into ships like cargo, stripped of their dignity, and treated as mere property, these men, women, and children endured unimaginable horrors. But their suffering didn't end upon reaching the shores of the so-called "New World." No, it only intensified as they were sold, brutalized, and forced to build the economy of a nation that saw them as less than human.

Public Enemy's song "Can't Truss It" captures this history's rage and pain. It's a sonic assault that demands attention: "Ninety damn days on a slave ship / Count 'em fallin' off two, three, four hun'ed at a time / Blood in the wood and it's mine / I'm chokin' on spit feelin' pain / Like my brain bein' chained." These lines cut to the core of America's hypocrisy, laying bare the exploitation and oppression that built this nation. This song is a powerful reminder that the roots of our systemic issues run deep, and their fruits are bitter. The "holocaust" I refer to isn't a relic of the past; it's "still goin' on."

But let's be clear: this book isn't just about the past. It's about the living, breathing legacy of that past. The chains of slavery may have been broken, but the shackles of systemic racism are still very much intact. From police brutality and mass incarceration to economic disparity and educational inequality, the echoes of the slave trade reverberate through every facet of American life. If you're not angry, you're not paying attention.

Enter Dr. Benjamin Chavis, a warrior in the ongoing battle for civil rights—a man who has faced down the beast of racism time and time again. Dr. Chavis's story is a testament to the relentless fight against oppression. Wrongfully imprisoned as one of the Wilmington Ten, he's experienced firsthand the corrupt systems that continue to suppress Black voices and lives. His leadership in the NAACP and work in environmental justice and economic empowerment are beacons of hope in this relentless struggle.

Dr. Chavis shows us that the fight against the legacy of the transatlantic slave trade is not just about seeking justice for past wrongs but about dismantling the present systems of oppression that have evolved from it. His life's work embodies the spirit of resistance and resilience, a hallmark of the African American experience. And, enter Stacy Brown, a freedom fighting journalist, whose work is renown and profound as he has demonstrated elite skills with his pen and a deft knowledge of his subjects.

This book doesn't pull punches. It dives deep into the atrocities of the transatlantic slave trade and lays bare the enduring impact on Black America. It's a raw, unfiltered look at the roots of racism and the ongoing fight for justice. It's about time we face this history head-on, without sugar-coating or sanitized narratives. This is about acknowledging the pain, the suffering, and the unyielding spirit of those who endured and resisted.

We need this book because too many still don't get it. Too many still turn a blind eye to the realities of our past and present. Too many still refuse to connect the dots between slavery and today's racial injustices. This book is a wake-up call, a demand for awareness, and a call to action.

It's about honoring the legacy of our ancestors by continuing their fight for true freedom and equality.

So, pick up this book and read it with an open mind and a heavy heart. Let it ignite your anger and fuel your resolve. Let it remind you that the struggle is far from over and that we all have a role in the fight for justice. This is not just a history lesson—it's a rallying cry.

In the words of Public Enemy, "Fight the Power." Educate yourself, challenge the status quo, and never stop pushing for the equality and justice that our ancestors fought and died for. This book is a weapon in that fight. Use it. And remember the message from "Can't Truss It"— don't trust the systems that oppress, don't trust the sanitized versions of history, and don't trust those who tell you that the fight is over. The struggle continues, and so must our resistance. We've got to get to the roots, never giving up, and always turning it loose. The story is "harder than the hardcore," and it's on us to carry it forward.

—CHUCK D

Preface

History reveals that whenever the denial of the oneness of all humanity is permitted, people sink into vicious, violent, and virulent acts of deprivation and dehumanization. Contemporary attempts to deny, ignore, justify, or condone the legacy of the centuries-long genocide and the international economic consequences of the Transatlantic Slave Trade (1500–2024) have to be resolutely challenged and refuted.

For over five hundred years, people and nations have been enriched by the impact and saddled with the contradictions of the Transatlantic Slave Trade. As a result of the international slave trade, unprecedented economic profits and wealth were acquired in Europe and in North and South America. Systemic social demonization, hatred, and prejudice; racial enslavement and oppression; geopolitical imperialism, massive mineral extractions, ethnic cleansing, and tribal warfare initiation and exploitation have all been carefully crafted, institutionalized, and embraced for over five centuries.

The brutal consignment and enforced categorization of African people as mere property devoid of any human attribution was part and parcel of the emergence of the haunted ideology of white supremacy. That derogatory ideology is still used today in an attempt to justify racism and inequity.

Distinctive in the annals of human history, the Transatlantic Slave Trade is ladened with evolving factual narratives that are stained with the blood of cruelty, injustice, and inhumanity. The following chapters bear witness to the depths of human suffering, the erosion of basic human dignity, and the resilient and transformative spirit that continues to endure even in the face of unimaginable prolonged adversity and oppression.

The Transatlantic Slave Trade: Overcoming the 500-Year Legacy is a contemporary testament, history, and documentation of events to empower our remembrance and reckoning and the possibility of reparations.

Comprising the research, reporting, and writings of the National Newspapers Publishers Association (NNPA); the Senior National Correspondent, Stacy M. Brown; and my own writings, research, and reflections, this volume illuminates the multifaceted dimensions of the transatlantic slave trade as a shared history. It is a mosaic woven from the threads of sorrow, resistance, and resilience—a literary work born from an award-winning series of writings observing the 500th anniversary year of the Transatlantic Slave Trade and its Abolition. In the U.S. this would occur in August 2019.

When Stacy Brown and I discussed doing this book together several years ago, we were profoundly aware of the demand and need for this compilation of facts and literary explication. At a time today when there are renewed efforts to burn and ban books about race and racial justice, we are grateful to find a publisher courageous enough to publish our findings and recommendations. We affirm—and believe—that truth is therapeutic.

Through meticulous research and a steadfast commitment to truth-telling, this volume delves into the facts that have lingered in the shadows of our collective consciousness for too long. Among published scholars on the subject of the transatlantic slave trade, there are today recurring debates and academic arguments about the importance of the quantitative versus the qualitative evidence that documents the terrorism of the evil vestige of human trafficking and profiteering.

We decided, however, that we should cover both the quantitative and qualitative manifestations as well as the subsequent impact of a continuing legacy of the enslavement of African people. One fact is irrefutable and must be noted. The transatlanticslave trade was the longest-running genocidal crime against humanity in world history, causing the death, enslavement, and suffering of over 60 million people from Africa, plus an additional 4 million descendants of Africa born into enslavement in North America and South America. Approximately a total of 30 million African people were enslaved for centuries in the Western Hemisphere.

Chapter one is the first of a series of award-winning articles reminding us that the United Nations recognized the imperative of preserving an accounting of the transatlantic slave trade—an act of commemoration that serves as a beacon, guiding us through the corridors of time to confront the harsh realities of the past and the promises of a better future.

Chapter two pierces the sanctum of faith, revealing the uncomfortable truth that religion played a pivotal role in the pseudo-justification of the slave trade. Even the Roman Catholic Church, an institution entrusted with the salvation of souls, was entangled in this long-term grievous enterprise. It is a stark reminder that the tendrils of complicity reached into the highest echelons of state power and moral authority.

In chapter three, we journey through five centuries—a span of time that stretches beyond the horizon of most historical narratives. Again, it is a shared history, an unbroken thread that binds continents, nations, and peoples in a tapestry of suffering, resilience, and eventual liberation.

Chapter four exposes the economic machinery that ran on the toil, sweat, and tears of the lives of the enslaved. It unravels the intricate web of commerce, profit, and exploitation underpinning the old empires and the birth of new nations—an economic legacy that continues to shape our world today.

"Are We Still Enslaved?" Chapter five poses a question reverberating through the ages. It is a poignant inquiry that challenges us to confront the vestiges of oppression that persist, sometimes insidiously, in the fabric of present-day society.

In chapter six, we delve into the roots of slavery, recognizing that its legacy extends far beyond the physical chains that once bound bodies. It is a legacy etched into the very psyche of nations throughout the modern and postmodern worlds, a haunting specter that lingers in the margins of humanity's collective global conscience.

Chapter seven bears witness to the tragic continuum—from enslavement to mass incarceration. It is a stark reminder that the shackles of inequality and injustice have shape-shifted but have not been fully cast aside.

Chapter eight unravels the threads of the struggle for civil rights and the insidious specter of environmental racism as we battle for equal justice in the realms of legislation as many of us face the toxicity we are disproportionately exposed to from discriminatory environmental policies affecting the air we breathe, the water we drink, the food we eat, the quality of the soil beneath our feet.

In chapter nine, we confront the stark reality that the echoes of the transatlantic slave trade still reverberate today throughout the African diaspora—a verification of the enduring scars etched into the collective memory of the systematic colonization and decolonization of African nations and peoples.

Chapter ten's invitation to the descendants of displaced peoples to "Come Home" appeals to all who want to reclaim their heritage stolen by the currents of history. It is an invitation to reconnect, rediscover, and repair and to heal.

Chapter eleven tells a remarkable tale of resilience—the story of an enslaved person whose knowledge of African medical science saved lives amid an epidemic. It is another truthful testament to the indomitable spirit of those who refuse to be extinguished, even in the most oppressive periods of human history.

In chapter 12, we unearth the roots of environmental racism and our haunting legacy by embarking on a riveting exploration of environmental racism's historical origins, and tracing back to the shadows of the transatlantic slave trade. The chapter unveils the enduring impact of systemic discrimination, exposing how marginalized communities bear a disproportionate burden of environmental hazards. Through gripping case studies and a call to action, we uncover the ongoing struggle for justice against a backdrop of historical inequities.

In chapter 13, we challenge preconceptions, dismantling the misleading myths surrounding black-on-black crime. We dive head-first into crime statistics, dissect societal structures, and unravel historical contexts to reveal a nuanced understanding of the complex factors contributing to crime in African American communities. This chapter demands a re-evaluation of ingrained stereotypes for a more informed discourse.

In chapter 14, we explore the widening wealth gap and decades of policy failures. Enter a world where the echoes of historical policies reverberate through the deepening wealth gap, particularly affecting those once enslaved. This chapter dissects systemic failures and policy shortcomings perpetuating economic disparities. With urgency, it calls for a comprehensive reexamination of economic policies to rectify the enduring consequences of slavery and systemic neglect.

Then, in chapter 15, we explore the fraught landscapes of redlining and gentrification, illuminating the systemic theft of opportunities and resources from communities of color. Readers can witness the urgency of confronting these discriminatory practices to halt further displacement and exploitation through historical revelations and contemporary examples. Brace yourself for a call to action against the silent erosion of marginalized populations.

In chapter 16, we scrutinize the news media's complicity in perpetuating racial biases and stereotypes. Through a critical lens on media coverage, representation, and framing, it unveils how racism is reinforced and amplified. This chapter presents a rallying cry for media literacy and reforms, demanding a more equitable and accurate portrayal of diverse communities in the unfolding narrative of our world.

The Slave Voyage Tracker and appendices A, B, C, and D serve as waypoints guiding us through the labyrinth of historical documents, resolutions, and declarations included in the magnitude of this shared history.

In the epilogue, we are graced by the wisdom and passion of African Union Ambassador Dr. Arikana Chihombori-Quao. Her address serves as a rallying cry, a call to action, and a reminder that the pursuit of justice is a collective endeavor transcending our borders.

We hold an unwavering conviction that remembrance, education, and commitment to truth may be further realized by those who are reached by this book. We affirm the attainable goal of forging a sustainable path to liberation, justice, equality, and economic equity—and a future where shadows of the past no longer hold sway over our present opportunities.

The future of the world will be greatly impacted by the steady progress of Africa's self-determination and the willingness of all nations and peoples to learn from the past.

My gratitude is especially owed to Stacy M. Brown for his integrity and fine character as he worked diligently to ensure the timely completion of this book using the power of his pen and commitment to the best of journalism and research. God bless.

BENJAMIN F. CHAVIS, JR.
Washington, D.C., June 2024

A Note to the Reader

In the following pages, we present a series of articles Dr. Chavis commissioned Stacy Brown to write to confront a history that is both painful and a chronicle of resilience—a testament to the human spirit's capacity to endure the worst of cicumstances—and against all odds rise up and transcend injustice. May this volume serve as a beacon of remembrance, a tribute to those who suffered, and a call to action for future generations.

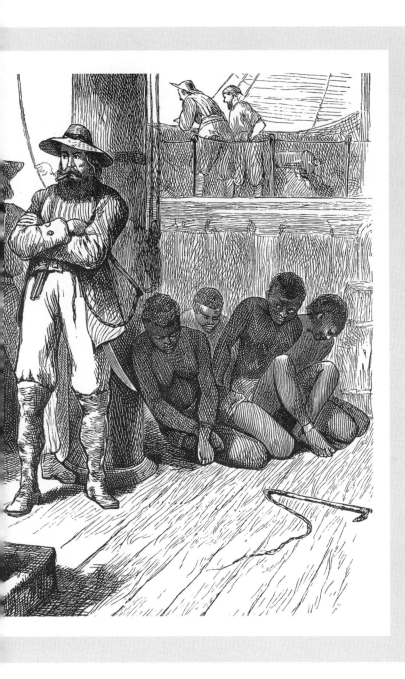

19th century print of slavers bringing
captives on board a slave ship
on Africa's west coast

71715 OLD SLAVE MARKET, CHARLESTON, S. C.

Old Slave Market, Charleston, South Carolina

CHAPTER ONE

The UN Observes International Remembrance of Slave Trade

"The fact that slavery was underway for a century in South America before the introduction in North America is not widely taught nor commonly understood..."

"A people without the knowledge of their past history, origin and culture is like a tree without roots."
—MARCUS GARVEY

In 2019, the National Newspaper Publishers Association (NNPA) announced the launch of a global news feature series on the history, contemporary realities, and implications of the transatlantic slave trade, according to NNPA President and CEO, Dr. Benjamin F. Chavis Jr. The following was their announcement:

> Under the President and CEO Dr. Benjamin F. Chavis Jr., and its Senior National Correspondent, Stacy M. Brown, the National Newspaper Publishers Association has taken a deeper look at the Transatlantic Slave Trade to further educate the world on the atrocities and aftermath of the most despicable and inhumane acts the world has ever witnessed. The National Newspaper Publishers Association (NNPA) is a trade association representing the more than 240 African American-owned newspapers and media companies in the United States, better known as The Black Press of America.

THE NIGHT OF AUGUST 22, 1791

The night of August 22 to the day of August 23, 1791, Santo Domingo, that changed its name to Haiti, and the Dominican Republic saw the beginning of the uprising that would play a crucial role in the abolition of the transatlantic slave trade.

The slave rebellion in the area weakened the Caribbean colonial system, sparking an uprising that led to abolishing slavery and giving the island its independence.

It also marked the beginning of the destruction of the slavery system, the slave trade and colonialism.

Each year, on August 23, the United Nations hosts an International Day for the Remembrance of the Slave Trade and its Abolition to remind the world of the tragedy of the transatlantic slave trade.

UN officials said it provides an opportunity to think about the historic causes, the methods, and the consequences of slave trade that must never be forgotten.

And, with the approaching 500th anniversary of the date Africans were first forced into slavery in America, many like Felicia M. Davis, the director of the HBCU Green Fund, which invests in sustainable campus solutions for historically black colleges and universities, said she believes African enslavement demands reexamination.

"The fact that slavery was underway for a century in South America before its introduction in North America is not widely taught nor commonly understood," Davis said.

"It is a powerful historical fact missing from our understanding of slavery, its magnitude and its global impact. Knowledge that slavery was underway for a century provides deep insight into how enslaved Africans adapted," Davis said.

Far beyond the horrific "seasoning" description that others have provided, clearly generations had been born into slavery long before introduction in North America, Davis argued.

"It deepens the understanding of how vast majorities could be oppressed in such an extreme manner for such a long period of time. It is also a testament to the strength and drive among people of African descent to live free," Davis told us..

The history of the United States has often been described as the history of oppression and resistance to that oppression, said David B. Allison, the editor of the book, *Controversial Monuments and Memorials: A Guide for Community Leaders.*

Slavery and the resulting touchstones stemming from slavery throughout the history of the United States run as a consistent thread that illuminates the soul and essence of America, said Allison, a historian with a master's degree in U.S. History from Indiana University-Purdue University at Indianapolis.

"From the compromises and moral equivocation in the founding documents during the Revolutionary Era—statements like 'All men are created equal' were written by a man who kept Black men and women as decidedly unequal as slaves—to the Civil War and Civil Rights Movement, the tragedy and terror of slavery are fundamental to the history of the United States," Allison said.

"Today, the fallout from the events of August 2017 in Charlottesville—brought about by a white supremacist rally and touching off the debate around the potential removal of a statute to a leader of the Confederacy—continue to weigh down the collective psyche of this nation," Allison continued.

"Moreover, the rise in police profiling and brutality of Black men and the resulting rates of incarceration for African Americans highlight the ongoing oppression that was initially born in the crucible of slavery," he said.

Allison added that it's "absolutely essential to understand and remember that 2019 is the 500th anniversary of slavery in the United States so that we can understand both how our country became how it is now and how we might envision a more just future for all citizens."

Each year the UN invites people from all over the world, including educators, students, and artists, to organize events for the International Day of Remembrance of Victims of Slavery & Transatlantic Slave Trade.

Theatre companies, cultural organizations, musicians, and artists take part on this day by expressing their resistance against slavery in performances that involve music, dance, and drama.

Educators promote the day by informing people about the historical events associated with slave trade, the consequences of slave trade, and the importance of justice to all and understanding our human rights.

Many organizations, including youth associations, government agencies, and non-governmental organizations, actively take part in the event to educate society about the negative consequences of slave trade.

"Here in America, many organizations, activists, and scholars are focused on 2019 as the anniversary of the arrival of the first Africans to be enslaved in Jamestown and marking 160 years since the last slave ship arrived," Felicia M. Davis said.

There's also a growing list of apologies for slavery from colleges and universities, local governments, and corporations.

Efforts are underway by the HBCU Green Fund to organize a national convening under the theme "Sankofa Remix" with three tracks: past, present, and future.

The goal is to examine history from an African American perspective, explore current impacts including backlash from the election of the first Black president, and crafting a vision that extends at least 100 years into the future that features presentations from artists, activists, technology, scholars, and other creative energy.

Felicia M. Davis told us, "It is encouraging to know that Black Press USA is focused on this topic. It is our hope that plans are underway to cover activities throughout the entire year, she said, noting that 2019 also marks the 100th anniversary of the Red Summer Race Riots. The UN Decade of African Descent 2015-2024 should also be highlighted as the Black Press USA leads this important examination of history."

Davis added, "Interestingly, the first and last slave ships to arrive in the U.S. both arrived in August. The HBCU Green Fund is working to put together a calendar of dates and observances. We would love to work with Black Press USA to promote a year-long observance that helps to reinvigorate and support the important role that the Black press plays in the liberation of Black people across the globe. We would be honored to have Black

Press USA as a Sankofa Remix partner organization and look forward to collaboration opportunities."

The transatlantic slave trade remains a pivotal, harrowing episode in human history, with profound and lasting impacts on individuals, societies, and nations. Exploring the United Nations' dedicated observance of this tragic event helps to shed light on the annual commemoration's objectives, significance, and global implications. Through initiatives aimed at remembrance, education, and collective responsibility, the UN addresses historical injustice while advancing the cause of human rights and equality. The transatlantic slave trade emerged in the 15th century, involving the forced transportation of millions of Africans to the Americas for labor under brutal conditions. It spanned over five centuries, with an estimated 12.5 million Africans forcibly transported.

With its annual observances, the United Nations openly recognizes that this resulted in profound demographic shifts and left an enduring cultural and socio-economic impact on the African continent and the Americas.

During observances, abolition movements are recognized, acknowledging that they gained momentum in the late 18th and 19th centuries, culminating in the abolition of the slave trade in the British Empire in 1807 and the United States in 1808. Because of United Nations observances, people around the globe are educated about international anti-slavery conventions, such as the Brussels Conference (1889-1890) and the League of Nations' Slavery Convention (1926), which marked early attempts at global cooperation against slavery.

In 2007, the United Nations General Assembly adopted Resolution 61/19, designating March 25 as the International Day of Remembrance of the Victims of Slavery and the Transatlantic Slave Trade. The date corresponds to the abolition of the British slave trade. The British Parliament passed the Abolition of the Slave Trade Act on March 25, 1807, making it illegal to engage in the transatlantic slave trade. That marked a pivotal moment in the global fight against slavery. The observance primarily serves as a platform to honor the memory of the millions of victims who suffered

and perished during the transatlantic slave trade. It emphasizes the importance of recognizing their humanity and the enduring impact on their
descendants. The UN said it aims to raise awareness about the historical
realities of the slave trade through educational initiatives, exhibitions, and
public events. This includes providing educational materials and resources
to facilitate a deeper understanding of this dark chapter in history.

During the observance, international figures reinforce the UN's
commitment to combating contemporary forms of slavery, such as human
trafficking, forced labor, and other exploitative practices. They join calls for
collective action to address the root causes and support survivors. Additionally, the United Nations Educational, Scientific, and Cultural Organization (UNESCO) plays a crucial role in developing educational materials
and resources focused on the transatlantic slave trade. It collaborates with
member states to incorporate accurate and comprehensive information
about this historical event into curricula at various educational levels.

There are also efforts to disseminate knowledge about the slave trade,
which face challenges such as the need for culturally sensitive and accurate representations and navigating political and social sensitivities
surrounding this topic. Nevertheless, UN and other officials agree that
effective educational initiatives contribute to a more informed and empathetic global citizenry. Meanwhile, member states actively contribute to
the UN's initiatives against modern forms of slavery. They participate in
formulating and implementing policies, legislation, and programs aimed
at preventing human trafficking, protecting victims, and prosecuting
perpetrators. Various international organizations, including non-governmental organizations (NGOs), intergovernmental organizations (IGOs),
and regional bodies, collaborate with the UN to fight against slavery.
These entities provide expertise, resources, and advocacy to complement
member states' efforts. Further, in recognizing the enduring legacies of
the slave trade, UN officials have said it is essential for understanding
and addressing contemporary forms of exploitation and discrimination.
This linkage underscores the necessity of ongoing vigilance and action to
combat modern-day slavery.

Most agree that knowledge of the Era of the Transatlantic Slave Trade provides a powerful lens to examine systemic inequalities and injustices. It highlights the interconnectedness of historical events with present-day disparities, emphasizing the need for comprehensive social and economic reforms. Acknowledging historical responsibility for the slave trade remains a contentious issue for some nations, UN officials have said. While some have issued formal apologies and reparations, others continue to grapple with the implications of their historical involvement. This debate underscores the complexities of reconciling past atrocities with present-day responsibilities. Striking a balance between commemorating the victims and taking meaningful, forward-looking action against contemporary forms of slavery also presents a challenge. Some argue that while remembrance is crucial, it must be coupled with concrete steps toward dismantling the structures perpetuating modern-day exploitation.

Several member states have implemented commendable initiatives to educate their populations about the transatlantic slave trade. For example, museums, memorials, and educational programs in countries like the United States, Brazil, and the United Kingdom serve as vital platforms for learning and reflection. Additionally, many countries have enacted legislation to combat modern forms of slavery, reflecting their commitment to the principles espoused by the United Nations. This includes laws addressing human trafficking, forced labor, other exploitative practices, and mechanisms for victim support and perpetrator prosecution. To ensure a sustained and impactful commemoration, the UN said efforts to strengthen educational initiatives should be prioritized, including expanding curriculum coverage, providing resources for educators, and leveraging digital platforms for broader accessibility.

The fight against modern slavery also necessitates continued international cooperation. The UN has said that member states and relevant stakeholders should collaborate to share best practices, improve cross-border law enforcement efforts, and address the root causes of human trafficking. The UN also promotes ongoing research on the slave trade and its contemporary implications, which they argue is crucial for a comprehensive understanding of this complex historical event. They also have encouraged academic engagement and supported research initiatives that would contribute to a more nuanced and informed discourse. Certainly, the United Nations' observance of the transatlantic slave trade is a testament to its dedication to human rights, historical remembrance, and eradication of all forms of slavery. It serves as a call to action for member states, organizations, and individuals to uphold the values of equality and justice. The observance not only honors the victims of the transatlantic slave trade but also reinforces the collective commitment to combat modern-day slavery. By remembering the past, the UN believes all are empowered to build a future free from exploitation.

CHAPTER TWO

The Catholic Church Played a Major Role in Slavery

"The universal church taught that slavery enjoyed the sanction of scripture and natural law."
—Dr. Jonathan Chism,
Assistant professor of history at the University of Houston-Downtown

"When the missionaries arrived, the Africans had the land, and the missionaries had the Bible. They taught us how to pray with our eyes closed. When we opened them, they had the land, and we had the Bible."

—Jomo Kenyatta, First President of Kenya, Africa

The Catholic Church played a vital role in the transatlantic slave trade, according to historians and several published theses on the topic.

The transatlantic slave trade was introduced by the coming of the Europeans who came with the Bible in the same manner that Arab raiders and traders from the Middle East and North Africa introduced Islam through the Trans-Saharan slave trade, according to AfricaW.com, a premiere informational website available throughout the continent.

"In fact, the Church was the backbone of the slave trade," authors write on the website. "In other words, most of the slave traders and slave ship captains were very 'good' Christians."

For example, Sir John Hawkins, the first slave-ship captain to bring African slaves to the Americas, was a religious man who insisted that his crew "serve God daily" and "love one another." His ship, ironically called "The Good Ship Jesus," left the shores of his native England for Africa in October 1562. Some historians argue that if churches had used their power, the Atlantic slave trade might have never occurred.

9

By the same logic, others argue that the Catholic church and Catholic missionaries could have also helped to prevent the colonization and brutality of colonialism in Africa. However, according to a 2015 Global Black History report, the Catholic church did not oppose the institution of slavery until the practice had already become infamous in most parts of the world.

In most cases, the churches and church leaders did not condemn slavery until the 17th century.

The five major countries that dominated slavery and the slave trade in the New World were either Catholic, or still retained strong Catholic influences including: Spain, Portugal, France, England, and the Netherlands.

"Persons who considered themselves to be Christian played a major role in upholding and justifying the enslavement of Africans," said Dr. Jonathan L. Chism, an associate professor of history and a fellow for the Center for Critical Race Studies at the University of Houston-Downtown.

"Many European 'Christian' slavers perceived the Africans they encountered as irreligious and uncivilized persons. They justified slavery by rationalizing that they were Christianizing and civilizing their African captors. They were driven by missionary motives and impulses," Chism said.

Further, many Anglo-Christians defended slavery using the Bible to support their claims. For example, white Christian apologists for slavery argued that the curse of Ham in Genesis Chapter 9 and verses 20 to 25 provided a biblical rationale for the enslavement of Blacks, Chism said.

In this passage, Noah cursed Canaan and his descendants, arguing that Ham would be "the lowest of slaves among his brothers" because he saw the nakedness of his father. A further understanding of the passage also revealed that while some have attempted to justify their prejudice by claiming that God cursed the black race, no such curse is recorded in the Bible.

That oft-cited verse says nothing whatsoever about skin color.

Also, it should be noted that the Black race evidently descended from a brother of Canaan named Cush. Canaan's descendants were evidently light-skinned—not black. "Truly nothing in the biblical account identifies Ham, the descendant of Canaan, with Africans. Yet, Christian apologists determined that Africans were the descents of Ham," Chism said.

Nevertheless, at the beginning of the sixteenth century, the racial interpretation of Noah's curse became commonplace, he said.

In 2016, Georgetown University in Washington, D.C. offered a public apology after acknowledging that 188 years prior to this time, Jesuit priests sold 272 slaves who were African Americans to save the school from financial ruin.

This is how *The New York Times* first reported the story: Jesuit priests in charge of the top Catholic university in the United States had received deliverance. But on that day, in the fall of 1838, no one else was spared from being sent away: not the 2-month-old baby and her mother, not the field hands, not the shoemaker and not Cornelius Hawkins, who was about 13 years old when he was forced onboard.

Their panic and desperation would be mostly forgotten for more than a century. But this was no ordinary slave sale. The enslaved African Americans had belonged to the nation's most prominent Jesuit priests. And they were sold, along with scores of others, to help secure the future of the premier Catholic institution of higher learning at the time, known today as Georgetown University.

"The Society of Jesus, who helped to establish Georgetown University and whose leaders enslaved and mercilessly sold your ancestors, stands before you to say that we have greatly sinned," Rev. Timothy Kesicki, S.J., president of the Jesuit Conference of Canada and the United States, said during a Liturgy of Remembrance, Contrition, and Hope.

"We pray with you today because we have greatly sinned and because we are profoundly sorry."

During the early republic, Catholics celebrated the new Constitution for its guarantee of religious liberty while simply accepting its guarantee of slaveholding, according to Blackthen.com.

Internal church politics mattered too. When the Jesuit order was suppressed in 1773, the plantation system of the order in Maryland was seen as a protection for their identity and solidarity.

The universal church taught that slavery enjoyed the sanction of scripture and natural law. Throughout the antebellum period, many churches in the South committed to sharing their version of the Christian faith with Blacks. They believed that their version of Christianity would help them to be "good slaves" and not challenge the slave system, Chism said.

"Yet, it is important to note that African Americans made Christianity their own, and Black Christians such as Nat Turner employed Christian thought and biblical texts to resist the slave system. Furthermore, Black and white abolitionist Christians played a major role in overturning the system of slavery," he said.

There's little doubt that for the majority of the past two millennia, Christian churches have grappled with the intricate issue of slavery, evolving from acceptance and participation in the slave trade to eventual disapproval and condemnation. The Oxford Bibliographies have meticulously chronicled the shifting ethical landscape of Christian slaveholding.

During the late ancient period, Christians, including churches, held other Christians in ownership without significant controversy. However, over time, Christian churches gradually began to prohibit this practice. By the early modern period, the ownership of fellow Christians became taboo, though illicit instances persisted. While select individuals, such as ministers and clergy members, raised questions about the legitimacy of slavery during this era, it wasn't until the 18th century that a minority of Christian churches began advocating for abolition, a stance that remained deeply divisive.

Throughout the early modern period, most Catholic and Protestant Christian churches endorsed and profited from slavery. Even the Quakers, renowned leaders in the abolitionist movement, took a century to expel enslavers from their congregations. In the United States, Christian denominations experienced schisms over the slavery issue in the 19th century. Christian ministers and missionaries constructed robust defenses of slavery grounded in Christian scripture and proslavery theology.

The most fervent abolitionists were the enslaved and the free Black Christians, who drew on scripture to bolster their anti-slavery and abolitionist convictions. Scholarly arguments have raged over whether Christian churches supported or opposed slavery. However, a substantial body of research has shed light on why enslaved people became Christians and how they skillfully used church structures to fight for their rights and protect their communities.

Much of this research has emanated from Latin America, where archival records are notably comprehensive. Still, significant studies also focus on Black churches in North America, particularly the pivotal role played by the African Methodist Episcopal (AME) and other African American-led churches. Scholars within this domain engage in lively discussions about the nature of conversion and the intricate interplay between African religions and Black Christianity.

Recent scholarship has underscored that Africans and their descendants were not passive recipients of Christianity; many actively sought baptism and leveraged church institutions as sanctuaries for themselves and their families. Another critical area of inquiry scrutinizes the interplay between the church, slavery, and race, illustrating how European Christians shaped racial categories while seeking to reconcile slaveholding with Christian doctrine.

As Christian nations ventured forth to establish empires across the Atlantic, the papacy condoned the enslavement of Africans under specific conditions. Protestant nations followed suit a century later, crafting their own colonial slave societies in the Americas, albeit with distinct laws and practices regarding slavery and Christianity.

The Making of New World Slavery: From the Baroque to the Modern, 1492–1800, Robin Blackburn's seminal work published in 1997, offers a sweeping overview of the evolving relationship between slavery and Christian churches within European empires, while Felicia M. Davis's seminal study in 1966 traces the trajectory of slavery from antiquity to the early modern era. Recent decades have witnessed a surge of interest in comprehending the church's history and slavery from the vantage points of non-Europeans, particularly Africans and Native Americans. Lamin Sanneh's 2006 essay "Christianity in Africa" and Richard Gray's 2012 analyses of Christianity in Africa highlight the crucial role that African Christians played, while Sylvester Johnson's comprehensive 2015 study,

African American Religions, 1500–2000, delves into the complex connections between African American religions, including Christianity, and racism, slavery, and colonialism.

Sylvia Frey and Betty Wood's 1998 survey stands as a pivotal exploration of African American Protestantism in the British Atlantic world. Kathryn Gin Lum and Paul Harvey's compilation in 2018 contains numerous essays germane to the study of religion, race, and slavery. Andrés Reséndez's 2016 work sheds light on the overlooked history of Native American enslavement, enriching our understanding of this complex historical nexus.

CHAPTER THREE

A Five-Hundred-Year-Old
Shared History

"It started with slave ships . . . There are more records of slave ships than
one would dream. It seems inconceivable until you reflect that for 200
years ships sailed carrying cargo of slaves. How can man be nonviolent . . .
in the face of the . . . violence that we've been experiencing for the past
(500) years is actually doing our people a disservice in fact, it's a crime,
it's a crime."
                              —PUBLIC ENEMY "Can't Truss It."

T he Transatlantic Slave Trade is often regarded as the first system
      of globalization and lasted from the 16th century through much
      of the 19th century. Slavery, and the global political, socio-eco-
nomic, and banking systems that supported it, constitutes one of the greatest tragedies in the history of humanity both in terms of scale and duration.

This was the largest mass deportation of humans in history and a determining factor in the world economy of the 18th century where millions of
Africans were torn from their homes, deported to the American continent,
and sold as slaves, according to the United Nations Educational, Scientific
and Cultural Organization (UNESCO).

The transatlantic slave trade that began about 500 years ago connected
the economies of three continents with Spain, Portugal, the Netherlands,
England, and France acting as the primary trading countries.

"The transatlantic slave trade transformed the Americas," wrote Dr.
Alan Rice, a Reader in American Cultural Studies at the University of
Central Lancashire in Preston in the United Kingdom.

"Three factors combined to cause this transformation. Large amounts
of land had been seized from Native Americans and were not being used,"

Rice said. "Europeans were looking for somewhere to invest their money and very cheap labor was available in the form of enslaved Africans [thus] the Americas became a booming new economy."

"The transatlantic slave trade also formed an essential bridge between Europe's New World and its Asia trade and, as such, it was a crucial element in the development of the global economy in the 18th century, " Professor Robert Harms wrote in Yale University's "Global Yale."

Harms, a professor of History at Yale and chair of the Council on African Studies continued: "There was one basic economic fact—little noticed by historians—that provides the key to the relationship between the direct trade and the circuit trade.

"When a French ship arrived in the New World with a load of slaves to be bartered for sugar, the value of the slaves equaled about twice as much sugar as the ship could carry back to France. For that reason, the most common form of slave contract called for fifty percent of the sugar to be delivered immediately and the remainder to be delivered a year later. The second delivery carried no interest penalty, and so the slave sellers were in effect giving the buyers an interest-free loan."

In total, UNESCO estimates that between 25 to 30 million people—men, women, and children—were deported from their homes and sold as slaves in the different slave trading systems. More than half, 17 million, were deported and sold during the transatlantic slave trade, a figure that UNESCO historians said doesn't include those who died aboard the ships and during the course of wars and raids connected to the slave.

The trade proceeded in three steps. The ships left Western Europe for Africa loaded with goods which were to be exchanged for slaves.

Upon their arrival in Africa, the captains traded their merchandise for captive slaves. Weapons and gun powder were the most important commodities but textiles, pearls and other manufactured goods, as well as rum, were also in high demand. The exchange could last from one week to several months.

The second step was the crossing of the Atlantic. Africans were transported to America to be sold throughout the continent. The third step connected America to Europe.

The slave traders brought back mostly agricultural products, produced by the slaves. The main product was sugar, followed by cotton, coffee, tobacco, and rice.

The circuit lasted approximately eighteen months and, in order to be able to transport the maximum number of slaves, the ship's steerage was frequently removed, historians said.

Many researchers are convinced that the slave trade had more to do with economics than racism. "Slavery was not born of racism, rather racism was the consequence of slavery," historian and West Indian scholar Eric Williams wrote in his 1994 book, *Capitalism and Slavery.*

"Unfree labor in the New World was brown, white, black, and yellow; Catholic, Protestant, and pagan. The origin of Negro slavery? The reason was economic, not racial, it had to do not with the color of the laborer, but the cheapness of the labor," Williams said.

Also, contrary to "the popular portrayal of African slaves as primitive, ignorant, and stupid, the reality is that not only were Africans skilled laborers, but they were also experts in tropical agriculture," said editor and social media and communications expert, Michael Roberts.

In a dissertation for Op-ed News.com earlier this year, Roberts said Africans were well-suited for plantation agriculture in the Caribbean and South America. Also, the high immunity of Africans to malaria and yellow fever, compared to white Europeans and the indigenous peoples of the Caribbean and South America, meant Africans were more suitable for tropical labor.

"While Native Americans' labor was initially used, Africans were the final solution to the acute labor problem in the New World. . . . The slave trade was one of the most important business enterprises of the 17th century. The undisputed fact is that the nation states of Europe stabilized themselves and developed their economies mainly at the expense of millions of Black African people," Roberts said.

During the 16th Century, when Europeans first made regular contact, West Africa had highly developed civilizations, and Africans were keen to trade their gold, silver, copper, Ivory and spices for European pots, pans, cloth, and guns. However, Europeans soon became more interested in exploiting the people of Africa and forcing them into slave labor.

Most of the slaves were taken from the West coast, but some were kidnapped further inland from the interior.

"The biggest lesson to be learned from this dark and evil chapter in human history is that exploiting fellow humans for cheap labor never pays off in the long run," said Pablo Solomon, an internationally recognized artist and designer who's been featured in 29 books and in newspapers, magazines, television, radio, and film.

"The acts of using fellow humans as beasts of burden to save a few bucks always ends up costing more in the long run both in real money and in societal decay," Solomon said.

"Any rationalization of misusing fellow humans is both evil and ignorant," he said.

One aspect of the transatlantic slave trade that would greatly enhance its understanding is that the English began to enslave and export Irish persons to the Caribbean in the time of Oliver Cromwell, said Heather Miller, an educator and writer with expertise in the teaching of reading and writing, who holds graduate degrees from Harvard and MIT.

Cromwell was known for his campaign in Ireland that centered on ethnic cleansing and the transportation of slave labor to Barbados.

"Irish enslaved persons worked alongside African enslaved persons in the Caribbean," Miller said.

However, historians generally agree that the most cruel and exploitative people have been the Africans.

"From the moment when Europeans took their slaves from a race different from their own, which many of them considered inferior to other human races and assimilation with whom they all regarded with horror, they assumed that slavery would be eternal," historian Winthrop D. Jordan wrote in his dissertation, "White Over Black: American Attitudes Toward the Negro."

While tribal leaders assisted in the capturing of some African slaves, it's without any doubt that foreigners were overwhelming the most egregious in their pursuit of men, women, and children who would be placed in the horrors of forced labor and inhumane treatment.

The transatlantic slave trade would become the largest forced migration in history. It started at the beginning of the sixteenth century and, until the mid-17th century, Spanish America and Portuguese Brazil were the major slave markets for European slave traders.

The Dutch participation in the transatlantic slave trade started in the 1630s and ended at the beginning of the nineteenth century, according to Henk den Heijer, professor emeritus in Maritime History at the Leiden University in the Netherlands. During that period, the Dutch shipped 600,000 Africans to the colonies in the New World.

"Initially, the Dutch were against slavery which was considered to be a catholic heresy. This antislavery point of view can be easily explained," den Heijer said.

"Dutch seafarers first ventured across the Atlantic without the intention of enslaving anyone. They were mainly interested in the trade in Atlantic products like salt, sugar, wax, and dyed wood. At the beginning of the 17th century, however, the Dutch established small plantation colonies on the coast of Guyana, the area between the Orinoco and Amazon rivers," he said. "Most of the early settlements were populated with Dutch colonists and a few indigenous slaves. The Dutch embraced the slave trade and slavery on a large scale for the first time in Brazil."

The slave trade also brought a great deal of wealth to the British ports that were involved. Researchers noted the count of slaves and slave ships that came through the main British ports in 1771, when the average working person earned $35 in British currency per year and a single slave in good condition could be sold in the Caribbean for $25. Liverpool had 107 ships and transported 29,250 slaves; historians noted.

London had 58 ships carrying 8,136 slaves while Bristol had 23 ships that transported 8,810 slaves. Additionally, researchers said Lancaster had 4 ships that transported 950 slaves.

From 1791 to 1807, British ships carried 52 percent of all slaves taken from Africa while, from 1791 to 1800, British ships delivered 398,719 slaves to the Americas.

While it was the British who stood as the most progressive couriers of whatever was transported through the sea, many other countries chartered ships and descended upon African nations to capture slaves.

Ships sailed to Africa loaded with guns, tools, textiles and other manufactured goods and crews with guns went ashore to capture slaves and purchase slaves from tribal leaders.

Slave ships spent months travelling to different parts of the coast, according to historians who describe the devastation of the transatlantic slave trade.

Captives were often in poor health from the physical and mental abuse they suffered.

The air in the hold was foul and putrid, according to historians. From the lack of sanitation, there was a constant threat of disease. Epidemics of fever, dysentery and smallpox were frequent. Captives endured these conditions for months. In good weather the captives were brought on deck in midmorning and forced to exercise.

They were fed twice a day and those refusing to eat were force-fed. Those who died were thrown overboard. The combination of disease, inadequate food, rebellion, and punishment took a heavy toll on captives and crew. Surviving records suggest that until the 1750s, one in five Africans on board ship died.

At least two million Africans—10 to 15 percent of those aboard—died during the infamous "Middle Passage" across the Atlantic.

Some European governments, such as the British and French, introduced laws to control conditions on board. They reduced the number of people allowed on board and required a surgeon to be carried out. The principal reason for acting was concern for the crew, not the captives, historians said.

The surgeons, often unqualified, were paid head-money to keep captives alive. By about 1800 records show that the number of Africans who died had declined to about one in 18.

When enslaved Africans arrived in the Americas, they were often alone, separated from their family and community, unable to communicate with those around them.

"When we arrived, many merchants and planters came on board and examined us. We were then taken to the merchant's yard, where we were all pent up together like sheep in a fold," according to a published description from *The Interesting Narrative of the Life of Olaudah Equiano.*

"On a signal, the buyers rushed forward and chose those slaves they liked best."

Sold, branded, and issued with a new name, the enslaved Africans were separated and stripped of their identity.

In a deliberate process, meant to break their will power and make them totally passive and subservient, the enslaved Africans were "seasoned," which meant that for a period of two to three years, they were trained to endure their work and conditions: Obey or receive the lash. It was mental and physical torture.

"The anniversary of the Transatlantic Slave Trade needs to be marked in some way, not celebrated, but recognized and memorialized because of the effects this decision had then that still affects the world today," said Dr. Jannette Dates, dean emerita at the School of Communications at Howard University in Washington, D.C.

"The Black Press continues to play its historic role in keeping issues of significance to African Americans in the forefront for black people's awareness, knowledge, and better understanding of our history," Dr. Dates said.

Helping to summarize the reality that the transatlantic slave trade began 500 years ago, new historical findings have continued to uncover the gruesome details of the inception of the Africa-to-America transatlantic slave trade marking exactly five centuries since its sinister origins. On August 18, 1518 (according to the modern Gregorian calendar), King Charles I of Spain issued a charter that authorized the direct transportation of enslaved people from Africa to the Americas.

So, while too many have accepted that the slave trade began 400 years ago, overwhelming evidence reveals proof that the horrific enslavement of Africans began a century prior to this—around 500 years ago.

Before the pivotal decree, dating back to at least 1510, enslaved Africans were primarily routed through Spain or Portugal before being further dispatched to the Caribbean. Charles's groundbreaking decision to establish a direct trade route between Africa and the Americas revolutionized logistics and propelled the scale and brutality of this heinous human trafficking industry.

Over 350 years, a staggering 10.7 million black Africans were forcibly transported across the Atlantic, leaving an additional 1.8 million souls to perish during the treacherous voyages. These revelations are a grim testament to the unimaginable suffering millions of Africans and their descendants endured.

The new insights into this book's chapter of slavery's dark history have been brought to light through meticulous research and a reexamination of archival records, shedding fresh perspectives on the unimaginable horrors that unfolded during the earliest years of the transatlantic slave trade.

Historians and scholars emphasize the imperative nature of acknowledging and confronting this grim legacy. Dr. Chavis, who wears many hats, including his role as a renowned historian specializing in African history, remarked, "These discoveries underscore the profound cruelty and inhumanity that underpinned the transatlantic slave trade. Understanding its origins is crucial to grapple with the enduring repercussions shaping our world today."

These revelations prompt calls for increased education and commemoration, ensuring that this historical harrowing period is neither forgotten nor downplayed. Educational institutions, museums, and cultural organizations are urged to integrate these previously unveiled details into their curricula and exhibitions to foster a deeper understanding of the lasting impacts of the transatlantic slave trade.

CHAPTER FOUR

The Economic Engine of the New Nation

"And America, too, is a delusion, the grandest one of all. The white race believes—believes with all its heart—that it is their right to take the land. To kill. Make war. Enslave their brothers. This nation shouldn't exist if there is any justice in the world, for its foundations are murder, theft, and cruelty. Yet here we are."

—COLSON WHITEHEAD, author of *The Underground Railroad*

O nce they reached the Americas, enslaved Africans were sold to the highest bidder at slave auctions and, once they had been purchased, slaves worked for nothing on plantations without any rights at all.

Often punished harshly, some slaves committed suicide. Pregnant women who were impregnated by their white slave masters often preferred abortion to childbirth in their situation.*

The historic accounts of the transatlantic slave trade only seem to worsen as they're told. From the earliest stages of the transatlantic slave trade 500 years ago and throughout that most ignominious period, few were able to escape. Most who attempted to flee were caught and beaten and some were even murdered.

Because punishment for Black peoples' outbursts against their White slaveholders was so severe, enslaved Africans tried to hide their acts of resistance—such as slowing down the pace of their work by pretending to be ill or breaking their tools or "accidently" causing fires.†

"Slavery is one of the foundational pillars of American society, propping up the nation in the earliest days of the Republic and touching the

---

* The master wished to reproduce": *The (Forced) Reproduction of Enslaved Life in the Antebellum South, 1808–1865*, by Aisha Djelid. https://blogs.reading.ac.uk/gender-history-cluster/2021/04/19/forced-reproduction/

† https://ldhi.library.cofc.edu/exhibits/show/hidden-voices/resisting-enslavement/day-to-day-resistance

lives of everyone in America," said Hasan Jeffries, a history professor at Ohio State University.

"And, its legacy has been long lasting," said Jeffries who, specializes in African American history and contemporary black history, which includes the institution of slavery and its effect on African Americans in the United States from the founding era through the Civil Rights movement and today.

"The deeply rooted belief in white supremacy that justified slavery survived its abolition in 1865 and undergird the new systems of African American labor exploitation and social control, namely Jim Crow, that sought to replace what had been lost as a result of emancipation," Jeffries continued. "Slavery may have ended in 1865, but a slaveholder mentality persisted, shaping the contours of American life for decades to come. This legacy of slavery is very much what African Americans have been fighting against from the moment of emancipation through the present."

James Madison's Montpelier estate on in Orange, Virginia, was the plantation and home of the Father of the Constitution where 300 enslaved men, women, and children worked on the grounds and attended to the Madison family. Now an institution that examines slavery during the Founding Era and its impact today, it recently commissioned a study that examined how Americans perceive their Constitutional rights.

Research determined that African Americans (65 percent) are less likely than whites (82 percent) to believe that their Constitutional rights are regularly upheld and respected.

The study also revealed that African Americans (62 percent) are more likely than whites (36 percent) to believe that civil rights are the most important Constitutional issue to the nation; these findings make it clear that race continues to play a major role in determining how Americans perceive Constitutional rights.

"Enslaved people were considered property during the Founding Era; therefore the Constitution's declarations of 'we the people' and 'justice' excluded them, protecting one of the most oppressive institutions in history," said Kat Imhoff, president, and CEO of James Madison's Montpelier.

"While the words 'slave' and 'slavery' are never mentioned in the Constitution, they are referenced and codified in a variety of ways throughout the document," Imhoff said.

"The founders compromised morality—many were recorded as being opposed to slavery, but on the other hand many were not, and power, in some cases the states, bowed to slaveholding counterparts to ensure the Constitution would be ratified in the name of economics," she said.

Imhoff continued: "Slavery, when all was said and done, was incredibly profitable for white Americans, and not just in the South. It was the economic engine of the new nation. While Madison and his ideas remain powerful and relevant, they also stand in stark contrast to the captivity and abuse of Madison's own slaves. At Montpelier, on the very grounds where Madison conceived ideas of rights and freedom, there lived hundreds of people whose freedom he denied."

Indeed, their story is one of the first in the continuing journey of Americans who struggled to throw off bonds of oppression and exercise the fullness of what it means to be free, Imhoff added.

Working at James Madison's Montpelier provides Imhoff a close view of slavery's legacy through the eyes of those who descend directly from the enslaved individuals who lived at Montpelier and other estates in the nearby Virginia area.

"As a leader of this cultural institution engaged in the interpretation of the studies of slavery, I believe to truly move forward, it is essential to engage the descendants to help us interpret slavery in real terms and illuminate their ancestors' stories," Imhoff said.

"Our country continues to grapple with the effects of slavery. Some of us feel it in deeply personal ways. Others only know of it historically or academically as part of the distant, long-ago past.

"These differences make it all the more important to engage in worthwhile discussions with each other. We must have a more holistic conversation about freedom, equality, and justice and ensure we are inclusive of those people whom it affects most readily."

The Jim Crow Era, a stark period in American history spanning from the late 19th century to the mid-20th century, remains a painful reminder of institutionalized racism. It was marked by systemic racial segregation, discrimination, and violence against African Americans, primarily in the Southern United States.

The term "Jim Crow" encapsulates a series of laws and practices enforcing racial segregation and discrimination. Its roots lie in the post-Civil War Reconstruction Era when efforts were made to rebuild and reshape the nation after the ravages of conflict. However, these efforts proved insufficient in safeguarding the rights of newly emancipated African Americans.

The shortfall of Reconstruction is evidenced in the fact that, despite the 13th, 14th, and 15th Amendments to the Constitution, which granted freedom, citizenship, and voting rights to African Americans, Southern states instituted "Black Codes" and other legal measures that restricted their civil and political liberties. Later, the end of Reconstruction saw a resurgence of white Democratic rule in the South. These "Redeemers" were determined to regain control from federal authorities, leading to efforts to disenfranchise African American voters. The 1896 Supreme Court decision in Plessy v. Ferguson, which validated "separate but equal" facilities, provided legal precedent for racial segregation in public spaces.

Several factors coalesced to give rise to the Jim Crow Era, including White Supremacy or the pervasive belief in white racial superiority fueled by the Jim Crow laws. Southern whites were resolute in maintaining social, economic, and political dominance. Unmasking White Supremacy remains an ongoing task in 2024. The enduring ideology continues to pose a significant challenge in contemporary society. Understanding its historical origins and the factors contributing to its persistence remains crucial in addressing this pressing issue.

The foundations of white supremacy can be traced back to the era of colonialism and the transatlantic slave trade. European powers justified their subjugation of non-white populations through a pseudo-scientific belief in racial hierarchies.

The aftermath of the American Civil War witnessed the emergence of white supremacist ideologies in the American South. Faced with the emancipation of enslaved people, many white Southerners sought to maintain their social, economic, and political dominance.

The Jim Crow Era was used to institutionalize racial segregation and discrimination, providing a legal framework for white supremacy in the Southern United States, and this period left a profound impact on race relations in the country.

Persistent economic disparities have played a significant role in perpetuating white supremacy. Racial wealth gaps, limited access to quality education, and job opportunities for marginalized communities contribute to the perpetuation of this ideology.

Institutionalized racism in various sectors, including criminal justice, education, and housing, has allowed white supremacy to persist. Unequal treatment and lack of access to resources disproportionately affect communities of color.

The rise of the internet and social media platforms has provided a platform for disseminating white supremacist ideologies. Online communities and forums have facilitated the spread of hate speech and extremist beliefs.

Political rhetoric that caters to white supremacist sentiments can further validate and encourage individuals who hold such views. Additionally, policies that disproportionately affect marginalized communities can reinforce existing racial hierarchies.

Further, the fear of demographic shifts, where white populations may no longer constitute the majority, can contribute to the persistence of white supremacist ideologies. Political and social narratives often stoke this fear.

Many an expert has said fostering a greater understanding of the historical roots and contemporary manifestations of white supremacy is crucial. Education can help dismantle misconceptions and challenge deeply ingrained beliefs.

Encouraging diverse representation in all aspects of society, from media to corporate leadership, helps challenge existing power structures and promotes inclusivity, as would implementing and enforcing policies that address systemic inequalities and discrimination. This includes criminal justice reform, anti-discrimination laws, and equitable access to education and economic opportunities.

Additionally, experts have said building strong, inclusive communities that actively combat hate and prejudice can be a powerful force against white supremacy. Community programs, dialogues, and partnerships can foster understanding and solidarity.

Recognizing the origins of white supremacy and the contributing factors is essential in dismantling this toxic ideology. Through education, policy reform, and community engagement, society can work toward a more inclusive and just future, free of white supremacy. Further obstacles that have hung around since Jim Crow include the Southern economy, which once relied on agriculture, mainly cotton, that hinged on African American labor. Segregation ensured strong white control over this labor force while preventing competition for jobs and economic opportunities.

Through literacy tests and poll taxes, white politicians effectively disenfranchised African American voters, consolidating their political power and enforcing discriminatory policies. The Jim Crow Era had deep and enduring effects on African American communities, including the stronghold segregation.

African Americans faced segregation in virtually all daily life, from schools and public transportation to restaurants and housing. Segregation perpetuated racial divides and entrenched inequalities. White supremacist groups, notably the Ku Klux Klan, committed violence and acts of terror against African Americans. Lynching, beatings, and intimidation tactics were employed to uphold white supremacy and instill fear in African American communities.

As if that wasn't enough oppression, economic opportunities for African Americans were severely limited. They were relegated to low-paying jobs with scant room for advancement. Economic oppression resulted in entrenched poverty in African American communities. Indeed, while the Jim Crow Era formally concluded with the Civil Rights Act of 1964, its legacy endures and can easily be discerned through disparities in educational opportunities initiated during the Jim Crow Era that persist today. African American students often contend with lower-quality schools and diminished resources in many parts of the country.

Economic disparities also endure. African Americans continue to face higher unemployment rates, lower wages, and restricted access to economic opportunities. The echoes of Jim Crow have reverberated in the dispro-portionately high rates of African Americans within the criminal justice system, where they often endure harsher sentencing and other unfair treat-ment. Although legal segregation is considered a thing of the past, de facto segregation persists in housing and education. Residential segregation continues to propagate disparities in opportunity and outcomes.

The effects of the Jim Crow Era, born of white supremacy, economic interests, and political maneuvering, inflicted deep scars on African Amer-ican communities, and for may it is everlasting. Its legacy, manifest in so many areas necessitates a steadfast commitment to rectifying historical injustices and forging a more equitable society. Understanding the roots, impact, and lasting effects of the Jim Crow Era is pivotal in pursuing a just and inclusive America.

CHAPTER FIVE

Are We Still Slaves?

"I prefer to be true to myself, even at the hazard of incurring the ridicule of others. Rather than to be false, and to incur my own abhorrence."

—FREDERICK DOUGLASS

"Ignorance is the greatest slave master in the universe . . . The greatest prison anyone can escape from is ignorance."

—MATSHONA DHLIWAYO

"These negroes aren't asking for no nation. They wanna crawl back on the plantation."

—MALCOLM X

Five Centuries ago—on August 18, 1518, to be exact—the King of Spain, Charles I, issued a charter authorizing the transportation of slaves direct from Africa to the Americas, according to the United Nations Educational, Scientific and Cultural Organization, or UNESCO.

Five hundred years later, the devastating effects remain.

Some argue, however, that slavery continues to exist, in that far too many African Americans possess a slave's mentality. Books on the topic are plentiful.

Harvard psychiatrist Alvin Poussaint wrote extensively about the high suicide rates among black males, which doubled over a 15-year period beginning in 1980. "African American young men may see the afterlife as a better place," Poussaint wrote in his book, *Lay My Burden Down: Suicide and the Mental Health Crisis among African Americans.*

In her book *Black Pain: It Just Looks Like We're Not Hurting*, famed author and social worker Terrie M. Williams writes about the "high toll of hiding the pain associated with the Black experience," the suffering from depression that led to her mission to help African Americans heal their emotional pain.

Portland State University scholar Joy DeGruy also tried explaining the slave mentality in her controversial theory, "Post-Traumatic Slave Syndrome."

The *Urban Dictionary* and other works say that "a slave mentality" is one of feeling inferior or of feeling lost without hope, a feeling that we do not have the power to significantly alter our own circumstances.

"Another sad symptom of having a slave mentality is believing that white people are superior," Kuuleme T. Stephens noted in her blog. "Persons can be conditioned to quietly, and without objection, accept harmful circumstances for themselves as the natural order of things. . . . They're also conditioned to accept the view of their 'master' and beliefs about themselves and strive to get others within their group to accept the same view."

"I often hear people make the claim that Blacks were better off when they were slaves. I have been known to say such things when people piss me off when they respond out of ignorance to a posting or article. My reason for making such an argument is if Black Americans are not going to stop living in the past and blaming others for their problems, we will never move forward as a people. . . . To maintain a belief that you are owed something and entitled to things when you are doing nothing to help yourself is absurd.

"To stay ignorant as a lifestyle choice and have others (the government) take care of you and tell you what to do is exactly what the slaves did, and some continued to do this even after they were freed. . . . My great grandmother, whose father and grandfather were slaves, has a slavery mentality because they were raised by slaves and their opinions and beliefs were passed down as such."

Even now, millions of Americans of recognizably African descent languish in societal backwaters, according to historians and experts on the effects of slavery. And the dichotomy that exists between those who view living in America as a struggle to survive and those that see it as a land of opportunity has driven a wedge between many in the African American community.

"We're absolutely still slaves today," said Sean XG Mitchell, a hip-hop activist and author of several books on the Black experience, including *The African American Spiritual Practice of Seven*.

"We're the only race of people who do not have a cultural orientation regarding our identity. Every powerful and successful race or ethnic group of people has an orientation that centers around language, education, religion, names, and customs, which is where their unity, self-respect, pride, and dignity—the prerequisite for power—comes from," he said.

As a result of slavery, African Americans do not have a cultural orientation that centers around their historical experience as a people. "We see the outcome in the deficiency of our social and economic development. To a certain extent, we've been fighting racism and injustice the wrong ways, which is why it's been an ongoing issue for over [500] years. Real empowerment comes from culture, and until we understand and embrace what it means to have origins in the black races of African people we will always be slaves," Mitchell said.

"I believe there is a dividing legacy of slavery that has pitted certain segments of the Black community against each other," Mitchell continued. "We have an obvious color barrier between light skin and dark skin, creating somewhat of a caste system that gives privilege to the lighter shade in most cases whether we're referring to employment opportunities or relationships."

"It's all a fallout of slavery because slaves often were pitted against each other as a means of preventing unity. During slavery, the dark-skinned blacks worked in the fields while light-skinned blacks worked in the house; hence the terms "field Negroes" and "house Negroes.""

"It got so bad, that not only did the slave owner, who was often responsible for the lighter shade of brown his slaves had, gave lighter-skinned Blacks more respect, but so did the dark-skinned Blacks," blogger Jasmyne Cannick writes in an opinion column for NPR.

This was best illustrated in Spike Lee's 1988 film *School Daze* in the scene set in a beauty salon between the "jiggaboos," the darker-skinned blacks with "nappy" hair, and the "wannabes," the lighter-skinned blacks with "straight" and often woven hair.

Cannick says, "You know, I can't think of one time that I witnessed or heard of White children taunting each other for being paler than another, but I can think of numerous occasions where I have seen Black children teasing each other for being 'too black.'"

"And while our lighter skin shades can be attributed to the massah's preference for his female Black slaves over his own wife, we can't blame the massah for us continuing to feed into the hype that light is good and dark is bad," she said.

Post-slavery, post-Jim Crow, and post-Civil Rights, African Americans haven't reached their full potential in part because of an acute lack of effort because too many wallowed in self-pity, say those who've argued against reparations.

Walter Williams, an economics professor at George Mason University in Washington, D.C. and an opponent of reparations, suggested that African Americans have actually benefited from the legacy of slavery.

"Almost every Black American's income is higher as a result of being born in the United States rather than in any country in Africa," Williams, who is Black, told ABC News.

"Most Black Americans are middle-class," Williams said, claiming that the U.S. has made "significant" investments in African Americans since the slave trade ended.

"The American people have spent $6.1 trillion in the name of fighting poverty," he said. "We've had all kinds of programs trying to address the problems of discrimination. America has gone a long way."

Countering that argument, others said America has continued to do a disservice to Black Americans, prolifically using the criminal justice system as tool akin to slavery that almost assures a lifetime of dependency on taxpayers.

"My expertise is the criminal justice system, which has long been used to intimidate, oppress, and abuse African Americans. While officially our laws today are color-blind, which is different from the time of slavery, our laws against discrimination are not always implemented," said Roy L. Steinheimer Jr., a professor of Law at Washington and Lee University in Virginia.

What about black-on-black crime?

According to an evidence brief from the Vera Institute of Justice titled "An Unjust Burden: The Disparate Treatment of Black Americans in the Criminal Justice System" and a report from the Bureau of Justice Statistics, most violence occurs between victims and offenders of the same race, regardless of the race.

The rate of both black-on-black and white-on-white nonfatal violence declined 79 percent between 1993 and 2015. The number of homicides involving both a Black victim and Black perpetrator fell from 7,361 in 1991 to 2,570 in 2016.

The issue isn't the crime; it's the selective disproportionately harsher punishment and sentencing of African Americans.

"Some of the laws, such as those disenfranchising convicted felons, have their origin, if not in the immediate aftermath of the civil war, then in the era that saw the emergence of the KKK and white supremacy. They were clearly intended to keep African Americans and likely, though to a lesser extent poor Whites, from the ballot box," Steinheimer said.

Meanwhile, some of the newer laws that have negatively affected African Americans still appear to result from some underlying beliefs that go back to the times of slavery.

"Interestingly that thinking has survived even during times of mass migration, which is presumably indicative of how deep-seated it is in American culture and law," the professor continued.

The "broad scope of the criminal justice system reinforces the wealth disparity between white and black by making those caught up in it ever poorer and serves to drive even some of the better-of people caught up in it into poverty," Steinheimer said.

"The economic impact resulting from slavery therefore gets magnified and reinforced by our criminal justice system, which increasingly stacks fines and fees," he said.

In a dissertation for the Brookings Institute, Glenn C. Loury wrote that the dream that race might someday become an insignificant category in our civic life now seems naively utopian.

In cities across the country, and in rural areas of the Old South, the situation of the Black underclass and, increasingly, of the Black lower working classes, is bad and getting worse. Simply put, the playing field has never been level for Black Americans and that has only worsened the mental health of the community. "No well-informed person denies this, though there is debate over what can and should be done about it," Loury said.

"Nor do serious people deny that the crime, drug addiction, family breakdown, unemployment, poor school performance, welfare dependency, and general decay in these communities constitute a blight on our society virtually unrivaled in scale and severity by anything to be found elsewhere in the industrial West," he said.

"Slavery is one of the foundational pillars of American society, propping up the nation starting in the earliest days of the Republic and touching the lives of everyone in America. And its legacy has been long lasting," said Hasan Jeffries, a James Madison Montpelier historian and history professor at Ohio State University who specializes in contemporary Black politics.

"The deeply rooted belief in white supremacy that justified slavery survived its abolition in 1865 and undergird the new systems of African American labor exploitation and social control, namely Jim Crow, that sought to replace what had been lost as a result of emancipation," Jeffries said.

As a result, slavery has caused certain symptoms of dysfunction in the African community, which has been reinforced in each generation, according to historians at the African Holocaust Network.

The legacy of slavery has promoted and nursed the direct association between being African and being inferior. Being African and being unequal. Being African and being incapable and less worthy.

It also promotes ways of thinking which continue to impede growth and development, such as cultivating dependence and reactive behaviors, and more content to be at best an observer complaining about the world, instead of being a change agent in the world.

"The deterioration of the Black American family is staggering," Stephens said.

"If you ask a young Black American what they want to be when they grow up, most will say they want to be a rapper/singer, football player, basketball player, or baseball player, and that is if they can tell you what they would like to be at all," she said.

"No one tells them that only 0.03 percent make it to pro basketball, 0.08 percent make it pro football, and 0.45 percent make it pro baseball.

"We have a 40 percent dropout rate, for every 100,000 Black men in the U.S., 4,777 are in prison or jail; for every 100,000 Black American women, there are 743 in jail or prison, and 72 percent of Black American women, and teens are unwed mothers."

Historians at the James Madison Montpelier in Virginia said that it's no accident that the U.S. Constitution opens with a message of inclusivity, establishing "justice" and ensuring "domestic tranquility" for the people.

However, it's what that most famous preamble—and, indeed, the rest of the document—doesn't address that's more telling: The Constitution's authors omit the vital distinction between their view of the differences between persons and property and, in doing so, ultimately protect one of history's most oppressive institutions: Slavery.

In a nation grappling with its historical sins, the trauma of enslavement continues to cast a long shadow over African Americans, manifesting in profound psychological and emotional wounds. Despite the urgent need for mental health support, the Equal Justice Institute noted that research shows that this community continues to underutilize therapeutic services.

Even when sought, the quality of care often falls short. Dr. Erica Wilkins, a distinguished expert in couple and family therapy, delved into the enduring impacts of slavery on African American couples and the therapeutic considerations for clinicians.

President Biden's recent proclamation of Juneteenth as a federal holiday marked a symbolic step towards acknowledging America's history. The nation has yet to fully recognize the direct line from chattel slavery to the forced labor endured in U.S. prisons today. Advocates have called for states to ratify the Abolition Amendment to address this grave injustice, thereby prohibiting forced labor under all circumstances.

The 13th Amendment, while abolishing slavery, paradoxically included a clause permitting its continuation as punishment for crime. This exception swiftly became a tool for exploitation, with Southern states implementing discriminatory Black Codes, targeting African Americans for trivial offenses like "vagrancy." These laws enabled Black individuals' incarceration and subsequent forced labor, further entrenching a system of oppression.

In a white paper, the Equal Justice Institute noted that in the 20th century the War on Drugs exacerbated this problem of racial targeting, leading to harsh sentences for non-violent drug offenses and a surge in the prison population. This action created a modern-day abomination, with nearly two million incarcerated individuals lacking protection from what amounts to legalized slavery. Disturbingly, a disproportionate number of these inmates are Black or are other people of color.

For incarcerated individuals, toiling under duress is a grim reality. Estimates suggest that a staggering $2 billion to $14 billion in wages is pilfered annually, benefiting private companies, state-owned entities, and correctional agencies.

In some Southern states, prisoners can be forced to work for nothing. Even in supposedly more progressive states, wages often amount to mere pennies daily. Refusing to work can lead to brutal consequences, including beatings, isolation, and restricted communication with loved ones.

The post-Civil War era known as Reconstruction initially held promise for newly emancipated Black citizens. Federal intervention was seen as crucial in safeguarding their rights, as many white Southerners resisted their newfound freedom. However, racial violence persisted, leaving many Black people vulnerable to systems controlled by their former oppressors.

The immediate aftermath of emancipation saw a surge in violence against African Americans across the South. This brutality served a dual purpose: forcing African Americans into labor and deterring them from leaving plantations. White supremacist groups like the Ku Klux Klan actively terrorized free Black people and their allies, leaving a trail of death and suffering.

Lynching emerged as a brutal tool of racial terror. A report in 2015 released by the Equal Justice Initiative (EJI) documented more than 4,400 lynchings that took place between 1877 and 1950. Researches in a June 2020 study, titled *Reconstruction in America: Racial Violence After the Civil War*, documents the number of nearly 6,500 Black people who died when lynched by White mobs during the end of the Civil War in 1865 to 1950.* These atrocities were not confined to the South. Over 300 documented cases occurred in non-Southern states. Lynchings and the systematic disenfranchisement of Black voters solidified white supremacy in the South.

The rewriting of Civil War history, divorcing it from its roots in slavery, perpetuated a distorted narrative. Efforts to memorialize Confederate leaders and erect monuments gained momentum, fueling a defiant brand of Southern identity. Even today, controversies surrounding Confederate symbols persist, underscoring the enduring impact of revisionism.

As the United States confronts its past, it must grapple with the continuing repercussions of slavery, racial terror, and segregation. Acknowledging this history is not merely an act of remembrance but a crucial step toward dismantling the persisting structural inequalities. Only through honest dialogue and concerted action can America reckon with its racial injustice legacy.

---

* https://eji.org/reports/reconstruction-in-america-overview/

CHAPTER SIX

The "Roots" of Slavery and Its Lasting Effects

Kunta Kinte: What's snow, Fiddler?

Fiddler: Never you mind, boy, never you mind. Let's get on back to home. I got enough trouble teaching you the difference between manure and massa. 'Course there ain't all that much difference when you gets right down to it.

The first time he had taken the massa to one of these "high-falutin' to-dos," as Bell called them, Kunta had been all but overwhelmed by conflicting emotions: awe, indignation, envy, contempt, fascination, revulsion—but most of all a deep loneliness and melancholy from which it took him almost a week to recover. He couldn't believe that such incredible wealth actually existed, that people really lived that way. It took him a long time, and a great many more parties, to realize that they didn't live that way, that it was all strangely unreal, a kind of beautiful dream the white folks were having, a lie they were telling themselves: that goodness can come from badness, that it's possible to be civilized with one another without treating as human beings those whose blood, sweat, and mother's milk made possible the life of privilege they led.

—ALEX HALEY, *Roots: The Saga of an American Family*

"I still have a dream. It is a dream deeply rooted in the American dream. I have a dream that one day this nation will rise up and live out the true meaning of its creed, 'We hold these truths to be self-evident, that all men are created equal.' I have a dream that one day on the red hills of Georgia, sons of former slaves and the sons of former slaveowners will be able to sit down together at the table of brotherhood. I have a dream that one day even the state of Mississippi, a state sweltering with the heat of injustice, sweltering with the heat of oppression, will be transformed into an oasis of freedom and justice. I have a dream that my four little children will one day live in a nation where they will not be judged by the color of their skin but by the content of their character."

—MARTIN LUTHER KING, JR.

T he year was 1976 and America was still feeling the aftershocks of the Civil Rights Movement, the murder, some eight years earlier, of Martin Luther King Jr., and the end of the Vietnam War.

King's death along with the murders of President John F. Kennedy and his brother, Senator Robert Kennedy—both of whom were proponents of civil rights and equal opportunity for African Americans and other minorities—were reminders to many that America still had not come close to achieving the slain leader's "Dream."

What's more, in 1976 journalist Alex Haley's sensational book *Roots: The Saga of an American Family* was published.

It would not only go onto become a best-selling book, but a much watched and talked about ABC Television mini-series that re-awakened everyone to the darkness, horrors, and inhumanity of the transatlantic slave trade.

"Alex Haley tapped into something very special, the idea that black Americans have been, are, and will always be compelled to understand their history," said Dr. Kellie Jackson, an assistant professor of Africana Studies at Wellesley University.

Jackson's research focuses on slavery, abolitionists, violence as a political discourse, historical film, and black women's history.

That *Roots* spawned an era where African Americans would give their newborn children African-themed names was no surprise and counts as an important moment in self-recognition, said Jackson, whose book, *Force and Freedom: Black Abolitionists and the Politics of Violence*, published in 2019 examines the conditions that led some black abolitionists to believe slavery might only be abolished by violent force.

"For many African Americans, giving their children names with meaning is incredibly important. What's remarkable about *Roots* is that despite the master's attempts to rename Kunta Kinte, 'Toby,' the name in popular culture and memory never stuck," Jackson said.

"Kunta Kinte is only referred to by his African name. I think this is a signal of the value African Americans place on names. In the 1970s and beyond, giving black children Afrocentric names provided not only a feeling of pride, but a sense of heritage in history."

Jackson continued: "Naming children after great rulers such as Nzinga, Kenyatta, or Chaka still resonates with many black parents today. I know parents who have given their children the name Obama. Names that are also signposts to historical moments. What's more powerful than your name?"

Still, those names come with a price because many agree that hate is as American as Apple Pie and baseball. And victims of such hate not only include the once enslaved African American. It's a country where it was once illegal for all women to vote.

It's a country that not only devastated Native Americans, but one with a long history of preventing those living on reservations to cast a ballot despite the historic amount of bloodshed and despair brought upon the original people who occupied their territory. Their state would demand requirements that impeded what is granted to them, such as not allowing them to vote in rural areas where people do not have residential addresses and receive their mail at a post office.

"I believe America owes Native Americans the chance to cast a ballot," said Shawn Halifax, a cultural history interpretation coordinator at the MacLeod Plantation Museum in Charleston, South Carolina. "I understand that what the law is and also that what people who are attempting to exercise their rights are told about the law can be two different things," Halifax said.

An article published in December 2023 about the voting of Native Americans stated:

"Colorado is poised to be the first state to expand automatic voter registration to Native American reservations, thanks to a new registration system.

Tribal members have the right to vote in elections, from the local to the national level, just like other U.S. citizens. But actually casting a ballot has been an uphill battle for many tribal residents, including those here in Colorado."*

America has always had a system of discrimination and prejudice against all groups who were not identified as "White Anglo-Saxon" native, said Walter Palmer, the founder of the Walter D. Palmer Leadership Learning Partners Charter School in Philadelphia and current faculty member at the University of Pennsylvania where he teaches urban studies and social policy and practice.

"Because historically American indigenous native's language, culture, history, customs and way of life has been wiped out and they have been a ward of the government, they lost their personhood," Palmer said of Native Americans.

"As American citizens, native indigenous people should be entitled to all the same privileges, rights and entitlements as all other American citizens," he said.

Palmer said America has continued to try and hold onto slavery, but in more legal forms like hate groups and prisons. "After the abolishment of slavery and the end of the reconstruction period, there was the rise of the Ku Klux Klan, which was a replacement of the slave patrols after this period."

"America always used the prison system as a means of threat, intimidation and social control and this was later enlarged to use Chain Gangs and Jim Crow laws to further control the African Americans," he said.

Palmer said, "*Roots* was built on the legacy of prior black historians and famous Black leaders over the past two hundred years, such as Fredrick Douglas, William B. Dubois, Booker T. Washington, Marcus Garvey, G. Carter Woodson, Martin Luther King, and Malcolm X.

"The connection that African Americans have had to the African Diaspora goes back to the "Back to Africa" movement of the early 19th

---

* https://www.rpbs.org/blogs/news/automatic-voter-registration-native-american-tribes/

century like the American Colonization Society that was created in 1821," Palmer said.

Halifax told us that for the 20th Century, *Roots* proved to be a watershed moment.

"I imagine it inspired an incredible number of people to seek to learn more about their family's past, because they knew little about it or had not been listening carefully to the stories of their elders," Halifax said.

"I think *Roots* strongly influenced some White Americans. I think the book helped place the notion in the minds of many Whites that enslaved populations were families and communities that experienced pain and suffering, that experienced joy and wonder, that were founders and builders of this country. That they were more than property," he said.

Halifax continued: "I think *Roots* helped usher changes regarding the placement of African Americans within the context of our national history. Of course, this did not happen just because of *Roots*.

"In fact, I think *Roots* was a crashing wave into America's consciousness that had been pushed by a swell generated during the Civil Rights and Black Power movements that preceded it. Stories from America's history to be highlighted as 'American History' for so long were decided by White male academics.

"I think *Roots* helped send a message that historians needed to be more inclusive in their storytelling. It was during the 70s and 80s that more inclusive social histories were being researched and pursued in academia, and academia began to become more diversified.

"By the 90s museums and historic sites began recognizing that there is more to America's story than just rich white guys, their families, and the wars they waged. And equally important it was by then that people began demanding more of these stories. Unfortunately, following the crashing wave of *Roots* there has been a very slow seep into the American conscious as a whole."

Evidence of its importance is in the fact that its remake as a mini-series in 2016 was the same year as the opening of the Smithsonian's National Museum of African American History and Culture," Halifax said.

"I suspect that was not an accident. We have a long way still to go. The study by the Southern Poverty Law Center on how slavery is taught in American schools is damning."

Halifax pointed out that it took 100 years for the National Museum of African American History and Culture to open. To lesser fanfare, and just before the opening of that museum on the National Mall, two other smaller museums opened within a few months of each other.

Both museums state that their purpose is to share the history of enslaved people and their descendants. Both are former slave labor camps, known euphemistically as plantations—the Whitney Plantation in Edgard, Louisiana, and McLeod Plantation Historic Site in Charleston, South Carolina.

"As far as I know they are the only two former plantation sites who have rejected the White-dominated narrative and look at these sites as places of memory for those held captive and enslaved and for those whose families survived," Halifax said.

"These two sites hold promise as places of healing where slavery, its legacy, and American racism can be examined. In the end, I think the novel *Roots* had an important and lasting impact."

Alex Haley's best-selling 1976 novel *Roots: The Saga of an American Family* that had won a Pulitzer Prize Special Citation award was an inspiration to many. It is widely acknowledged that the miniseries *Roots* that aired on ABC represented a watershed point in the history of American television. The television series followed the journey of an African slave named Kunta Kinte and his descendants over the course of several decades.

When *Roots* first aired on January 23, 1977, it immediately won the hearts and minds of people all around the United States and the rest of the world. It had a significant impact on society, bringing up controversial topics such as racism, identity politics, and the lingering effects of slavery. The Black Press investigated the impact that the television series *Roots* had not only on the United States but also on the rest of the world by analyzing the historical, cultural, and social climate both before and after the series debuted.

The 1970s was a decade that saw substantial social and political shifts in the United States. The Civil Rights Movement of the 1960s had made progress toward removing racial segregation and discrimination, but entrenched disparities continued to exist even after the many successes achieved. The Vietnam War, that was still going on at the time, was a very divisive conflict causing substantial anti-war demonstrations and a societal divide.

A significant number of Americans had been left disillusioned and suspicious of those in authority because of the Watergate affair that led to the unprecedented resignation of an American president. The scandal surrounding Richard Nixon further damaged people's trust in government institutions. Amid all these changes, the television miniseries *Roots* emerged as a potent catalyst for conversations about race, identity, injustice, and the aftereffects of slavery.

When the first episode of the *Roots* mini-series aired, it was nothing short of a cultural earthquake. According to estimates, 130 million people watched it, meaning more than half of the American population followed the broadcasts. The series served as a powerful example of the potential of television as a platform for presenting significant stories and the cultural reflection on those stories. Alex Haley's *Roots* pushed the envelope of what was considered acceptable in the entertainment industry by providing a depiction of the African American experience that was uncompromising. Its influence was felt far beyond the bounds of the screen, as passionate conversations about the serious subjects it raised were held in homes, classrooms, and workplaces worldwide.

The popularity of *Roots* challenged the established standards of television production. Before the series premiere, portrayals of African American history and slavery were sometimes simplified or exaggerated for dramatic effect. Alex Haley's *Roots* sought a higher standard of truth and authenticity, pushing the boundaries of what could be accomplished in the genre of historical storytelling on television. That dedication to telling the truth ushered in a new era of television programming that sought to confront complex social topics with authenticity and depth.

There's little doubt that *Roots* acted as a jarring reminder of the violence and dehumanization that enslaved Africans were forced to endure throughout that period. The frank depiction of history pushed American citizens to face the unsettling realities of their nation's history. It became a rallying point for efforts to confront the historical injustices and systemic inequalities that continue to exist in our society today.

Additionally, *Roots* sparked a significant increase in people interested in African ancestry and family history. A lot of people saw Alex Haley's trip to learn his family history, and it motivated them to go on their own adventures of self-discovery. The African American community developed a stronger sense of cultural belonging and pride as a result of this search for their roots, which became an undertaking that was both intensely personal and communal.

Roots gave African Americans a strong awareness of their shared cultural heritage. It was a celebration of the resiliency and fortitude of a community of people that had triumphed over tremendous obstacles. This solidarity manifested in increased political engagement as communities fought for legislative changes that addressed systemic injustices and promoted social justice.

The influence of *Roots* was felt well beyond the borders of the United States. It exposed a global audience to the history of slavery in the United States, thanks to its broadcast in more than 50 nations. The series sparked debates on topics of racial inequality, discrimination, and human rights in countries all over the world.

CHAPTER SEVEN

From Enslavement to Mass Incarceration

"The genius of the current caste system, and what most distinguishes it from its predecessors, is that it appears voluntary. People choose to commit crimes, and that's why they are locked up or locked out, we are told. This feature makes the politics of responsibility particularly tempting, as it appears the system can be avoided with good behavior.

But herein lies the trap. All people make mistakes. All of us are sinners. All of us are criminals. All of us violate the law at some point in our lives. In fact, if the worst thing you have ever done is speed ten miles over the speed limit on the freeway, you have put yourself and others at more risk of harm than someone smoking marijuana in the privacy of his or her living room. Yet there are people in the United States serving life sentences for first-time drug offenses, something virtually unheard of anywhere else in the world."

—MICHELLE ALEXANDER,
The New Jim Crow: Mass Incarceration in the Age of Colorblindness

"We live in the most incarcerated country in the world. There are more black men under correctional control today than there were under slavery in 1850."

—JOHN LEGEND, Singer, song writer, and pianist

The United States has just five percent of the world population yet holds approximately 25 percent of its prisoners.

From the beginning of the transatlantic slave trade, slavery deprived the captive of legal rights and granted the master complete power. Millions of slaves in America were humiliated, beaten, and killed while black families were torn apart.

Slavery was abolished in 1865 with the end of the Civil War and passing of the 13th Amendment, but America found what many see as a disingenuous way of continuing its slave master ways—mass incarceration.

The NAACP recently released statistics revealing that in 2014, African Americans constituted 2.3 million, or 34 percent, of the total 6.8 million correctional population.

African Americans are incarcerated at more than five times the rate of whites and the imprisonment rate for African American women is twice that of white women.

Nationwide, African American children represent 32 percent of children who are arrested, 42 percent of children who are detained, and 52 percent of children whose cases are judicially waived to criminal court.*

Though African Americans and Hispanics make up approximately 32 percent of the U.S. population, they comprised 56 percent of all incarcerated people in 2015.†

If African Americans and Hispanics were incarcerated at the same rates as whites, prison and jail populations would decline by almost 40 percent, according to the NAACP.‡

"Five hundred years after the transatlantic slave trade, the strife and hate that remains is largely due to miseducation. To date, there has not been an honest evaluation accepted by the general public about the true relationship between African people in America and the European settlers, typically referred to as just Americans," said activist and television personality Jay Morrison.

"This is one of the reasons that I wrote my book, *The Solution: How Africans in America Achieve Unity, Justice and Repair*. In it, there is informative dialogue on the true experience of Africans in America during the enslavement era, the post-enslavement era, and current day America— which I refer to as the 'mass incarceration era.' Most Americans choose to live blindly and accept the political oppression, economic exploitation, and social degradation of Africans in America," Morrison said.

"The longing by blacks for independence often threatens and offends many Americans and many people don't believe in African Americans' right to liberation and cannot fathom their desire to be in their true and original state, often leading to a fight," he said.

---

* https://naacp.org/find-resources/history-explained/origins-modern-day-policing
† Ibid.
‡ Ibid.

"I believe there is an opportunity in this millennial-led age to get past the hate if there is true atonement. Until America can take full responsibility for its past and correct what is still purposefully occurring—mass incarceration, the school-to-prison pipeline, unequal school systems, gentrification, police brutality—the tension will continue to exist," Morrison said.

He continued: "Until all people can be honest about our history and lack of repair, the hate will be hard to get past. These human rights violations against Africans in

America must be treated with the same seriousness as other communities that have experienced similar imprisonment, oppression, exploitation, and genocide. When that playing field is levelled, I imagine a greater peace in America."

Added Je Hooper, of the American Ethical Union and the Brooklyn Society for Ethical Culture said: "The Black, Brown, and beige community continues to seek a remedy for their post-traumatic slave syndrome, particularly in a time of a socio-political climate that is fueled by discriminatory political rhetoric, violent sensationalized media, and disjointed cultural information.

"Our country has lived in fear because of its own nationalist amnesia. I feel we must rise to the occasion for communities of color to unapologetically shine," Hooper said.

The Legacy Museum: From Enslavement to Mass Incarceration in Montgomery, Alabama, dedicates its efforts to educate Americans and others about the transatlantic slave trade and its ties to mass incarceration.

The Equal Justice Initiative opened the 11,000-square-foot museum on April 26, 2018. It was built on the site of a former warehouse where enslaved Black people were imprisoned. This location is midway between an historic slave market and the main river dock and train station where tens of thousands of enslaved people were trafficked during the height of the domestic slave trade. In 2021, the museum was enlarged to hold larger exhibits and an art gallery. The stunning National Memorial for Peace and

Justice and the outdoor Freedom Monument Sculpture Park were also erected in Montgomery and have many visitors.

Montgomery's proximity to the fertile Black Belt region, where slave-owners amassed large enslaved populations to work the rich soil, had elevated Montgomery's prominence in domestic trafficking. By 1860, Montgomery was the capital of the domestic slave trade in Alabama, one of the largest slave-owning states in the United States.

According to Bryan Stevenson, the founder, and Executive Director of the Equal Justice Initiative in Montgomery, a narrative of racial differences was created to justify the brutal, dehumanizing institution of slavery in America.

Stereotypes and false characterizations of Black people were disseminated to defend their permanent enslavement as "most necessary to the well-being of the Negro"—an act of kindness that reinforced white supremacy, Stevenson said.

"The formal abolition of slavery did nothing to overcome the harmful ideas created to defend it, and so slavery did not end; it just evolved," he said.

In the decades that followed, these beliefs in racial hierarchy took new expression in convict leasing, lynching, and other forms of racial terrorism that forced the exodus of millions of Black Americans to the North and West, where the narrative of racial difference were manifested in urban ghettos and generational poverty.

Racial subordination was codified and enforced by violence in the era of Jim Crow and segregation as the nation and its leaders allowed Black people to be burdened, beaten, and marginalized throughout the 20th century, according to the officials of The Legacy Museum and the Equal Justice Initiative.

Progress towards civil rights for African Americans was made in the 1960s, but the myth of racial inferiority was not eradicated.

Black Americans were vulnerable to a new era of racial bias and abuse of power wielded by our contemporary criminal justice system.

Museum officials said mass incarceration has had devastating consequences for people of color. At the dawn of the 21st century, It was projected that one in three Black boys would go to jail or prison in his lifetime.

"Our nation's history of racial injustice casts a shadow across the American landscape," Stevenson said. "This shadow cannot be lifted until we shine the light of truth on the destructive violence that shaped our nation, traumatized people of color, and compromised our commitment to the rule of law and to equal justice."

The Equal Justice Initiative in Montgomery is committed to ending mass incarceration and excessive punishment in the United States, to challenging racial and economic injustice, and to protecting basic human rights for the most vulnerable people in American society, Stevenson said.

"I know the 13th Amendment provides the means for the criminal justice system to continue the practice of institutional slavery in the United States, for it is very clearly stated, 'Neither slavery nor involuntary servitude, except as a punishment for crime whereof the party shall have been duly convicted, shall exist within the United States, or any place subject to their jurisdiction. Congress shall have power to enforce this article by appropriate legislation,' said Shawn Halifax, a cultural history interpretation coordinator at the Charleston County Park and Recreation Commission in Charleston, South Carolina.

"There is plenty of evidence since its passage that individual states and the United States have chosen to exercise the entirety of this amendment to the constitution and have manipulated the institution of criminal justice to make it happen," Halifax said.

In the United States, a nation that proudly upholds the ideals of freedom and justice, lies a profoundly troubling phenomenon of mass incarceration. Rooted in a complex history of policies and practices, this issue has disproportionately affected African American communities, perpetuating a cycle of oppression that traces back to the nation's early days.

The roots of modern American policing can be traced to 1838, when Boston established the nation's first formalized police force. Many in Black communities believe the officers were slave catchers on a mission to retrieve runaway slaves, though American law enforcement disputes that claim. Ultimately designed to address urban disorder and theft, the role of police forces has evolved significantly over time. As America grappled with racial segregation and civil rights issues, law enforcement became a tool to enforce these deeply divisive policies.

For instance, The War on Drugs, launched in the 1970s and 1980s, ostensibly aimed to combat drug abuse and trafficking. However, in practice, it targeted African American communities with devastating consequences. Mandatory minimum sentences for drug-related offenses led to an alarming surge in incarceration rates, particularly for nonviolent drug offenses. The punitive measures caused generations to suffer, neighborhoods to become unstable, and families to split apart. The penalties were reminiscent of slavery when owners sold off family members, separating husbands and wives, mothers and daughters, fathers and sons, and siblings.

The 1990s Crime Bill, signed into law in 1994, addressed rising violent crime rates. Yet, it inadvertently worsened the issue of mass incarceration, allocating substantial resources for prison construction and hiring more police officers. Moreover, the bill imposed mandatory minimum sentences for certain offenses, contributing further to the burgeoning prison population.

The impact of mass incarceration on African American communities remains staggering. Despite representing only about 13 percent of the population, African Americans constitute a disproportionate 37 percent of the incarcerated population. And the percent of people serving life, life without parole, or "virtual life" sentences who are Black is 48% +. This glaring disparity results from systemic biases within the criminal justice system, including racial profiling and sentencing disparities.*

For many, release from incarceration does not end their struggle. Limited access to employment, housing, and education impedes their ability to reintegrate into society. This cycle of incarceration perpetuates a cycle of disadvantage, imposing long-lasting hardships on individuals, families, and communities.

---

* https://www.prisonpolicy.org/research/race_and_ethnicity/

The parallels between mass incarceration and the history of racial oppression in the United States are stark. Dating back to the days of slavery, the criminal justice system was utilized to target and control Black communities. With the abolition of slavery, the rise of convict leasing and the Black Codes continued this tradition, effectively re-enslaving many African Americans under a different guise.

In the present day, mass incarceration dismantles families, robs individuals of economic opportunity, and perpetuates cycles of poverty. African Americans, who have borne the brunt of this crisis, still face significant hurdles in their pursuit of justice and equality.

Reforming sentencing laws to focus on rehabilitation, rather than solely on punishment, is vital. Investment in education and economic opportunities for marginalized communities can disrupt the cycle of incarceration. Community-based alternatives to incarceration, such as drug treatment programs and mental health services, can address the root causes of criminal behavior. And most crucially, comprehensive reforms are needed to eradicate racial profiling and biased policing practices

In unraveling the tangled web of mass incarceration, American must confront the origins of our deep-seated biases and their profound effects on marginalized communities. By doing so, the nation can strive for a future where the ideals of freedom and justice indeed ring true for every American.

Large group standing in front of buildings on Smith's Plantation,
Beaufort, South Carolina, 1862

CHAPTER EIGHT

From Slavery to Civil Rights and Environmental Racism

"There is simply no denying the difference in response to predominantly black compared to predominantly white communities."

—FELICIA DAVIS,
founder and CEO of the HBCU Green Fund and
sustainability director at Clark Atlanta University

"In the end, the slave trade left the continent underdeveloped, disorganized, and vulnerable to the next phase of European hegemony: colonialism."

—MAHDI ADAMU

"The Delivery of Slaves from the Bight of Benin in the Eighteenth and Nineteenth Centuries," in H.A. Gemery and J.S. Hogendorn, *The Uncommon Market: Essays in the Economic History of the Atlantic Slave Trade*

"Racism is still with us. But it is up to us to prepare our children for what they will have to meet, and, hopefully, we shall overcome."

—ROSA PARKS

"Environmental racism is the deliberate targeting of ethnic and minority communities for exposure to toxic and hazardous waste sites and facilities, coupled with the systematic exclusion of minorities in environmental policy making, enforcement, and remediation."

—DR. BENJAMIN F. CHAVIS JR., 1981

*M*illions of able-bodied individuals were captured and transported from their African homes in the era of transatlantic slave trade. A large number of the enslaved were destined to remain in Africa. Many were transported across the Sahara to the north, which heightened the impact of the slave trade on the continent. It is estimated that the population of Africa remained stagnant until the end of the nineteenth century.

The death toll from the economic and environmental destruction caused by wars and slave raids was startlingly high. During the famines that followed military actions, the old and very young were often killed or left to starve. Forced marches of the captives over long distances also claimed many lives.

Besides its demographic toll on the continent, slave trade and the resistance to it led to profound social and political changes. Social relations among Africans were restructured, and their traditional values were subverted. This resulted in the development of predatory regimes, as well as regression in many communities.

Often African communities relocated as far from the slave trade routes as possible. In the process, their technological and economic development was hindered by their need to devote their energy to hiding from danger and defending themselves.

The disruption was immense. Relationships among kingdoms, ethnic groups, religious communities, levels of castes, rulers and subjects, and the enslaved and the free, were transformed. In some decentralized societies, people evolved new styles of leadership that led to more rigid, hierarchical structures thought to ensure their protection.

In addition, European powers intervened in the political process to prevent the rise of centralized African states that would have hampered their operations.

It was decades ago when in 1987 a Civil Rights leader, Dr. Benjamin F. Chavis Jr., who now serves as president and CEO of the National Newspaper Publishers Association, coined the term, "environmental racism."

It not only proved to be an apt term, for the circumstances but it harkens back to centuries of demoralization of Black Americans since the beginning of the transatlantic slave trade 500 years ago.

Once the slave trade ended, other oppressive eras ensued: The Antebellum Period, The Dred Scott Decision, The American Civil War, Jim Crow laws to systemize racism against Black people, and Racial Terrorism and throughout the 20th and 21st centuries, Environmental Racism, which has kept an immovable wedge between African Americans and the rest of Americans.

In noting that environmental justice is an important part of the struggle to improve and maintain a clean and healthful environment—particularly for African Americans who have traditionally lived, worked, and played closest to the sources of pollution—Chavis said that environmental racism is racial discrimination in environmental policy making and the unequal enforcement of the environmental laws and regulations.

"It is the deliberate targeting of communities with people of color for the placement of toxic waste facilities and officially sanctioning the use of life-threatening poisons and pollutants," he said. "It is also manifested in the history of excluding people of color from leadership in the environmental movement."

With President Donald Trump castigating the science of global warming, there's little wonder that today's environmental policies not only target people of color when it comes to the placement and operation of unhealthy facilities; they also exclude people of color from being a part of the policy making process—even though they are the ones who are usually most directly negatively impacted by environmental injustices.

"The underlying message of environmentally racist tactics and strategies is that certain neighborhoods and certain people matter less than others, and that geographical vulnerability is inevitable, when in fact it is socially constructed to be this way," said Dr. Deborah J. Cohan, an Associate Professor of Sociology in the Department of Social Sciences at the University of South Carolina Beaufort.

"The message is that some groups of people and some neighborhoods are okay to be dumped on and treated as garbage. After all, garbage is trash; it is what we've decided we no longer need or have any use for," said Cohan, who also writes for *Psychology Today* and *Teen Vogue*.

Cohan continued: "It's what we wish to dispose of as we have decided it has no value. The problem with racism and society's response to it is that we have failed to see this most basic thing: that in order to do that much damage to a community, one must so thoroughly objectify and dehumanize the people in it that they become things that can be discarded and forgotten about. People's ability to thrive under these hostile conditions is greatly compromised."

While many celebrated the end of Scott Pruitt's time as head of the Environmental Protection Agency, others argued that his brief tenure could have a lasting impact on marginalized communities dealing with poor health, water contamination, or air pollution, because of environmental injustice.

And Trump's policies revealed that the president himself cares little, if at all, about environmental racism.

Studies have shown that black and Hispanic children are more likely to develop asthma than their White peers, as are poor children, with research suggesting that higher levels of smog and air pollution in communities of color is a factor. A 2014 study, as reported by VOX, found that people of color live in communities that have more nitrogen dioxide, a pollutant that exacerbates asthma.

The EPA's own research further supported this. Earlier this year, a paper from the EPA's National Center for Environmental Assessment found that when it comes to air pollutants that contribute to issues like heart and lung disease, Blacks are exposed to pollutants 1.5 times more than Whites, while Hispanics were exposed to about 1.2 times the amount of pollutants than non-Hispanic Whites. People in poverty had 1.3 times the exposure of those not in poverty. Even with these assessments, under Pruitt enforcement of laws at the EPA has dropped considerably, with civil rights cases suffering in particular.

"Environmental racism is real. As documented in Richard Rothstein's 2017 book, *The Color of Law,* extensive federal, state, and local government practices designed to create and maintain housing segregation also assured those polluting facilities like industrial plants, refineries, and more were located near Black, Latino, and Asian American neighborhoods," said Bruce Mirken, a spokesman for The Greenlining Institute, a public policy advocacy group in Oakland, California.

"Extensive data show that low-income communities of color still breathe the worst air and have excessive rates of pollution-related illnesses like asthma and other respiratory problems," Mirken said. "These problems won't fix themselves. . . . As we move away from oil, coal, and gas to fight climate change, we must consciously bring clean energy resources and investment into communities that were for too long used as toxic dumping grounds. Here in California, The Greenlining Institute and allies have made considerable progress in designing our state's climate policies to focus on underserved communities. Such efforts need to be increased and expanded nationwide."

What's more, a scan of environmental boards, C-suites, foundations, campaigns, and funding, reveals a pronounced lack of diversity within the environmental movement that results in a White progressive worldview that still values science and the physical landscape more than people—especially black and brown people—according to Felicia Davis, founder and CEO of the HBCU Green Fund and sustainability director at Clark Atlanta University.

"These communities are also less affluent and more likely to be located near environmental hazards and to experience environmental dangers. Actions during Katrina and the crisis of lead in the municipal drinking water in Flint, Michigan, exemplify environmental racism addressed by environmental justice advocates," said Davis, who's the author of *Air of Injustice* and serves on the boards of Green 2.0, The Chattahoochee River Keepers, and the National Coalition on Black Civic Participation.

Davis is also a U.S. Representative for the global networking organization Gender CC: Women for Climate Justice and has traveled internationally to participate in numerous United Nations World Conferences on Climate Change.

"There is simply no denying the difference in response to communities that are predominantly Black compared to predominantly white communities," Davis said.

"In spite of a growing focus on diversity, equity, and inclusion, race remains an identifiable factor that impacts both access to opportunity, information, and resources. This is a subtle systemic challenge referred to as institutionalized racism, and the outcome is limited investment in environmental justice organizations," she told us.

Davis continued: "Since environmentalists are generally progressive, they sometimes target impacted communities under an environmental justice banner. Local or indigenous leadership is often under-valued with outsiders funded to address issues for or with impacted communities. That this approach is not even considered inherently flawed is further evidence of how these communities are regarded."

Chavis also noted Trump's declaration that climate change isn't real. "The same people in high political positions that deny the truth of the science about climate change are the same people who deny the factual history and current manifestations of racism," Chavis said. "Environmental racism is real, as is climate change."

CHAPTER NINE

The Transatlantic Slave Trade: 500 Years Later the Diaspora Still Suffers

"Impossible is just a big word thrown around by small men who find it easier to live in the world they've been given than to explore the power they have to change it. Impossible is not a fact. It's an opinion. Impossible is not a declaration. It's a dare. Impossible is potential. Impossible is temporary. Impossible is nothing."
—MUHAMMAD ALI

"We need to exert ourselves that much more and break out of the vicious cycle of dependence imposed on us by the financially powerful: those in command of immense market power and those who dare to fashion the world in their own image."
—NELSON MANDELA

*M*uch of the wealth generated by the transatlantic slave trade supported the creation of industries and institutions in modern North America and Europe. The most enduring consequences of the migration for the migrants themselves, and for the receiving communities, were the development of racism and the corresponding emergence and sustenance of an African American community, with particular cultural manifestations, attitudes, and expressions.

The legacy is reflected in music and art, with a significant influence on religion, cuisine, and language, according to Paul E. Lovejoy, a distinguished research professor and Canada Research Chair in African Diaspora History at York University in Toronto.

"The cultural and religious impact of this African immigration shows that migrations involve more than people; they also involve the culture of those people," Lovejoy said in a recent post about the creation of the African diaspora.

American culture is not European or African but its own form, created in a political and economic context of inequality and oppression in which diverse ethnic and cultural influences both European and African—and in some contexts, Native American—can be discerned, Lovejoy said.

"Undoubtedly, the transatlantic slave trade was the defining migration that shaped the African Diaspora. It did so through the people it forced to migrate, and especially the women who were to give birth to the children who formed the new African American population," he said.

These women included many who can be identified as Igbo or Ibibio but almost none who were Yoruba, Fon, or Hausa.

Bantu women from matrilineal societies also constituted a considerable portion of the African immigrants, and it appears that females from Sierra Leone and other parts of the Upper Guinea Coast were also well represented, Lovejoy said.

"These were the women who gave birth to African American culture and society," he said.

After many rang in 2019 with celebratory parties and gatherings, there were still others who solemnly recalled the beginning of the transatlantic slave trade that started 400 years ago—or 500 years, depending upon the region.

For Africans throughout the diaspora, their struggle not only traces back 400 or 500 years, but continued and was underscored as recently as 135 years ago when the infamous Berlin Conference was held.

The conference led to the so-called "Scramble for Africa" by European powers who successfully split the continent into 53 countries, assuring a division that remains today.

"There isn't a single thing that was more damaging to Africa than the Berlin Conference," said African Union Ambassador Dr. Arikana Chihombori-Quao.

"Africans weren't even invited to the conference," she said.

At the conference, which took place over three months in Brazil beginning in February 1884 and was attended by 13 European nations and the United Sates, ground rules were established to split Africa.

"Africans are still suffering the consequences," the ambassador said.

John W. Ashe, the president of the United Nations General Assembly said:

"The Transatlantic slave trade for 400 to 500 years deprived Africa of its lifeblood for centuries and transformed the world forever."

"There's no question that legacies of the slave trade persist today in most of the countries Africans were taken to," said Ayo Sopitan, founder of Pendulum Technologies in Houston, Texas.

"I have been thinking about how Africans and the diaspora need to get together—through proxies in the persons of recognized leaders—and have a conversation about the past, the role that African collaborators played, and how we can unite as a people. Then, and only then, will we be able to excel as a people," Sopitan said.

"I have sat at lectures by Henry Gates and learned about blacks in the Americas. The conclusion is that wherever we are, Blacks are usually at the bottom of the totem pole. This does not have to continue," he said.

The transatlantic slave trade was an oceanic trade in African men, women, and children that lasted from the mid-sixteenth century until the 1860s. The great majority of captives were collected from West and Central Africa and from Angola, according to the United Nations Educational, Scientific, and Cultural Organization (UNESCO).

Before the first Africans arrived in British North America in 1619, more than half a million African captives had already been transported and enslaved in Brazil. By the end of the nineteenth century, that number had risen to more than 4 million.

The trade was initiated by the Portuguese and Spanish especially after the settlement of owners of sugar plantations in the Americas, UNESCO officials noted in a 2018 web presentation titled, "Slavery and Remembrance."

Northern European powers soon followed Portugal and Spain into the transatlantic slave trade. European traders loaded African captives at dozens of points on the African coast from Senegambia to Angola and around the Cape to Mozambique.

European planters spread sugar throughout the Caribbean that was culti-vated by enslaved Africans on plantations in Brazil and later in Barbados.

In time, planters grew other profitable crops, such as tobacco, rice, coffee, cocoa, and cotton with European indentured laborers as well as African and Indian slave laborers.

Nearly 70 percent of all African laborers in the Americas worked on plantations that grew sugarcane to produce sugar, rum, molasses, and other byproducts for export to Europe, North America, and elsewhere in the Atlantic world, according to UNESCO.

The majority of African captives were carried to their destinations by the Portuguese, Brazilians, British, French, and Dutch. British slave trad-ers alone transported 3.5 million Africans to the Americas, UNESCO reported.

The transatlantic slave trade was complex and varied considerably over time and place, but it had far-reaching and lasting consequences for much of Europe, Africa, the Americas, and Asia.

The profits gained by Americans and Europeans from the slave trade and slavery made possible the development of economic and political growth in major regions of the Americas and Europe.

Europeans used various methods to organize the Atlantic trade. Spain licensed (by Asiento agreements) other nations to supply its Span-ish American and Caribbean colonies with African captives. France, the Netherlands, and England initially used monopoly companies.

In time, the demand for African laborers in the Americas was met by more open trade that allowed other merchants to engage in the trade with Africans.

As a result, formidable private trading companies emerged, such as Britain's Royal African Company (1660–1752) and the Dutch West India Company of the Netherlands (1602–1792), according to UNESCO.

The profits generated from the Atlantic trade economically and politically transformed Liverpool and Bristol in England, Nantes and Bordeaux in France, Lisbon in Portugal, Rio de Janeiro and Salvador de Bahia in Brazil, and Newport, Rhode Island, in the United States.

Each port developed links to a wide hinterland for local and international goods in Asia and capital to sustain the trade in African captives.

European merchants and ship captains—followed later by those from Brazil and North America—packed their sailing vessels with local goods and commodities from Asia to trade on the African coast.

Enslaved Africans, their often violent capture and enslavement out of sight of the European general public, were exchanged for iron bars, textiles, luxury goods, cowrie shells, liquor, firearms, and other products that varied from region to region over time.

Much of the wealth generated by the transatlantic slave trade supported the creation of industries and institutions in modern North America and Europe.

To an equal degree, profits from slave trading and slave-generated products funded the creation of fine art, decorative arts, and architecture that continues to inform aesthetics today, UNESCO officials said.

"European countries—Portuguese, English, French, and Spanish—were the most complicit in the transatlantic slave trade. This pernicious form of slavery was driven by European capitalistic countries seeking to expand their nation-states and empires," said Dr. Jonathan Chism, assistant professor of history and a fellow with the Center for Critical Race Studies at the University of Houston Downtown.

The hurt to many continues today.

"The fact that slavery was underway for a century in South America before its introduction in North America is not widely taught nor commonly understood," said Felicia Davis of the HBCU Green Fund.

"It is a powerful historical fact missing from our understanding of slavery—its magnitude and global impact. Knowledge that slavery was underway for a century [before it began in North America] provides deep insight into how enslaved Africans adapted," Davis said.

She continued: "Far beyond the horrific seasoning description, clearly generations had been born into slavery long before their introduction in North America. It deepens the understanding of how vast majorities could be oppressed in such an extreme manner for such a long period of time," Davis said. "It is also a testament to the strength and drive among people of African descent to live free."

Africa, the cradle of humanity, stands at the nexus of history, culture, and struggle. Its legacy from the transatlantic slave trade continues to shape the continent today, echoing the complex relationship between Africans and Black Americans, the persisting specter of neocolonialism, and the enduring impact of slavery. This article ventures deeper into these dynamics, uncovering the intricacies of Africa's present reality.

The transatlantic slave trade, a chapter of unparalleled brutality, permanently frazzled Africa's collective memory. Millions were torn from their homelands, yet the African spirit endured. Those who survived forged a legacy of strength that permeates the continent's rich tapestry of cultures and traditions.

Descendants of these survivors, dispersed across the globe, form the African diaspora. Among them, Black Americans share a profound connection with their African roots, giving rise to a dynamic interplay of shared heritage and distinct experiences.

The aftershocks of slavery reverberate through African societies, impacting every facet of life. Economic disparities, caste systems, and deeply entrenched social divisions persist, a testament to the profound scars of centuries of exploitation.

Communities in regions with heavy slave trade legacies often grapple with a complex blend of cultural amalgamation and preservation. In the Americas, remnants of African cultures persist in language, religion, and art, forging a unique fusion of traditions that is both a testament to survival and a tribute to resilience.

The end of formal colonial rule did not signal the cessation of exploitation. Neocolonialism, a subtler form of domination, continues to seep through economic, political, and cultural channels. African nations often find themselves ensnared in unequal trade relationships, debt burdens, and resource extraction schemes that hamper their ability to chart their own course.

France's relationship with its former African colonies exemplifies this neocolonial dynamic. Pegged to the Euro, the CFA Franc grants France significant sway over economic policies in 14 African nations. Critics argue that this arrangement perpetuates dependency, stifles economic self-sufficiency, and maintains an imbalance of power.

In Francophone Africa, the legacy of colonialism intertwines with the present. Former French colonies struggle with the lingering influence of their former colonizer despite their economic and political ties. Attempts to break free from this dynamic often face resistance as nations seek to assert their autonomy while navigating complex histories.

The CFA Franc, viewed by some as a symbol of ongoing economic subjugation, remains a focal point of debate. Calls for currency reform and greater financial independence continue reverberating through Francophone Africa.

The connection between Africans and Black Americans is multifaceted, steeped in shared history and distinct experiences. Both communities grapple with systemic racism and inequality, yet cultural, linguistic, and geopolitical factors shape their respective identities.

While cultural exchanges and collaborations are on the rise, the complexity of this relationship remains. While rooted in a shared heritage, historical narratives, unique journeys, and evolving cultural expressions all contribute to a dynamic society

Africa today grapples with a legacy that is both a testament to resilience and a reminder of ongoing challenges. A rich history of survival illuminates the continent's future path, from the scars of slavery to the complexities of neocolonialism and the diaspora dynamic. By acknowledging these complexities and forging meaningful partnerships, Africa can chart a course toward a future defined by empowerment, equity, and prosperity for all its inhabitants.

CHAPTER 10

The Transatlantic Slave Trade— Africans Urged to 'Come Home'

"A people without the knowledge of their past history, origin, and culture is like a tree without roots."

—MARCUS GARVEY

"For Africa to me . . . is more than a glamorous fact. It is a historical truth. No man can know where he is going unless he knows exactly where he has been and exactly how he arrived at his present place."

—MAYA ANGELOU

The Transatlantic Slave Trade started with slave ships, whips, chains, and a most demonic kind of evil: Europeans and others hunting down Africans like animals.

In the 1480s, Portuguese ships were transporting Africans to work as slaves on sugar plantations in the Cape Verde and Madeira islands in the eastern Atlantic.

Spanish conquistadors took African slaves to the Caribbean after 1502, and Portuguese merchants continued to be active in the transatlantic slave trade for another century and a half, operating from their bases in the Congo-Angola area along the west coast of Africa.

During the 17th century the Dutch became the primary slave traders. In the century that followed, British and French merchants controlled about half of the transatlantic slave trade, taking a large percentage of their human cargo from the region of West Africa between the Senegal and Niger rivers, according to Britannica.

Probably no more than a few hundred thousand Africans were taken to the Americas before 1600. However, in the 17th century, demand for slave labor rose sharply with the growth of sugar plantations in the Caribbean and tobacco plantations in the Chesapeake region of North America. The largest numbers of slaves were taken to the Americas during the 18th century, when, according to historians' estimates, nearly three-fifths of the total volume of the transatlantic slave trade took place.

The result was that an estimated 12 million enslaved Africans were shipped as cargo across the Atlantic Ocean to the Americas between the 16th and 19th centuries—and, according to the *Encyclopedia Britannica*, that figure represented just one stage of the slave trade.

Today, as the world takes note of the anniversary of the slave trade [500 years for some, 400 for others], a rousing call has gone out to Africans throughout the diaspora. "Everyone agrees that all that is needed for Africa to take her rightful place on the world stage is for her children to come back home," said Her Excellency Dr. Arikana Chihombori-Quao, the African Union Ambassador to the United States of America.

Celebrities, including Boris Kodjoe, Idris Elba, and Naomi Campbell, traveled to Ghana to visit The Akwamuhene Odeneho Kwafo Akoto III at the Bogyawe Palace, Akwamuhene, where he has conferred a citation for "leading our kinsmen home."

"My special thanks go to Boris Kodjoe and his colleagues for coordinating this all-important trip which I believe is by divine design," The Akwamuhene said.

"Today forms part of the new awakening. The beginning of our joint resolve to create a continent that we can all feel pride in calling our ancestral home. In many ways, we are grateful for the opportunity to heal and grow together as people united by both blood and purpose."

Ghana's President H.E. Nana Akufo-Addo reportedly planned several events for 2019 in commemoration of the anniversary of the transatlantic slave trade. The commemoration began with the "Full Circle Festival" which brought numerous celebrities and others who visited historical sites and attended a breakfast hosted by the president.

The festival was established to honor African ancestry by celebrating the continent's heritage and generational legacy. The "Coming Home" theme was expected to continue throughout the year.

"This celebration of 'Coming Home' is one that should be encouraged and promoted across the global black community," said Roman Debotch, owner and contributor of the website, Black Excellence, a platform used to shed light on noteworthy achievements in the Black community.

"I hear time and time again from black Americans who traveled to Africa about how connected they felt and how different they found whatever country they traveled to from the images of Africa they grew up with," Debotch said.

"The transatlantic slave trade still has an effect on the Black community in America and 'Coming Home' should show and teach Black Americans that their history doesn't begin as slaves," she said.

"There is a rich and vibrant culture and history that took place centuries before and after the transatlantic slave trade. Although they might feel cut off from it, it is at least a good move to visit these countries and know what exists there," Debotch said.

Jeanette Brown, founder of Excellence & Presence Communications, said going back to Africa means an invitation to return to where her ancestors are from. "It cancels out all the negative images I grew up seeing on TV and the stereotypes that African Americans are not welcomed in Africa, as we are 'not the same,'" Brown said.

Further, "returning to Africa should mean that there's a resurgence in wanting to know history, and it's a movement that will bring everyone of African ancestry together as opposed to further separating them," she said.

"Yes, the transatlantic slave trade effects still reach down today. The effects become more apparent the more we learn and uncover," Brown said. "The more we are educated on our history we will be able to unpack our similarities and differences. We should also be careful of who is sharing our history with us."

Brown continued: "In 2019, we are still learning about our origins. Crimes are still being labeled 'the worst in history'. . . and none of those statements end with 'transatlantic slave trade.' The invite home is a way for me to support my brothers and sisters. If we understand where we come from, we will know where we can go."

Marketing executive turned actor/filmmaker, Shantel Moses said she recently performed a "23-and-Me DNA Test" which revealed her African heritage.

Moses, who describes herself as African Caribbean American, lives in Brooklyn, N.Y., and said she now feels a greater urgency to visit Africa. "I've traveled to over 40 countries, heavily concentrated in Europe and Latin America. It's now time for me to come home," Moses said.

"Programs to entice people of African Heritage are super critical to help bridge the gap within the diaspora, whether we are African American, Afro Latino, Afro Australian—the power and beauty of us as Black people holds special power that can be leveraged by the continent," she said.

"I don't know what I will feel when I go home, but I can't wait to do so. I'm hoping to go to Ethiopia in 2019. While my roots are more in the West African region—I'm 34 percent Nigerian—I eagerly await the joy of touching down on my ancestors' soil."

CHAPTER 11

A Slave's African Medical Science Saves Lives of Bostonians During the 1721 Smallpox Epidemic

"I didn't know I was a slave until I found out I couldn't do the things I wanted."

—FREDERICK DOUGLASS

"I am not ashamed of my grandparents for having been slaves. I am only ashamed of myself for having at one time been ashamed."

—RALPH ELLISON

Every Black History Month, the observance of Black Excellence, Black Girl Magic, Black Power, and other invigorating movements of African Americans begin to take center stage.

From Dr. Martin Luther King Jr. to Malcolm X and many of the world's greatest Black athletes and entertainers, the country celebrates their achievements.

While some may never tire of hearing about the greatness of Civil Rights leaders, famous black athletes, and renowned entertainers, Black History Month also represents a time to focus on the unsung.

"I'd like to read about people who made impacts but are not entertainers, musicians, and those we hear about every Black History Month," said Kisha A. Brown, the founder and CEO of Justis Connection, a service that connects the top legal talent of color to local communities.

"The Black Press is an aspect of the fabric of the Black existence in America that is not getting enough attention or support from the community. We rally to support athletes and artists who are 'wronged' by the system, but we fail to honor is the voice of the Black Press that has been capturing our stories for centuries," Brown said.

"Long before Black Twitter and online blogs, and so the Black Press is not only an essential voice, but it is also a historical and cultural archaeological goldmine that we must preserve," she said.

In an email, Laurie Endicott Thomas, the author of *No More Measles: The Truth About Vaccines and Your Health*," said the most important person in the history of American medicine was an enslaved African whose real name we do not know.

"His slave's name was Onesimus, which means useful in Latin. The Biblical Onesimus ran away from slavery but was persuaded to return to his master," Thomas said.

"The African American Onesimus was the person who introduced a practice of immunization against smallpox to North America. This process was called variation because it involved giving people a serum containing viral substance from patients who had a mild form of the smallpox. Variation led to sharp decreases in the death rate from smallpox and an important decrease in overall death rates," she said.

Thomas' thoughts jelled with a Harvard University study and a Boston WGHB report by Edgar B. Herwick III in 2016 noting that after 150 years, Jack Daniels finally came clean that its famed whisky recipe arrived courtesy of a Tennessee slave.

Thomas told a story of a famous slave named Benjamin Bradley born in 1830 was owned by a slaveowner in Annapolis, Maryland. When he showed he had great skills in mechanical engineering, his master arranged for him to learn to read and write at the Naval Academy and was given some small jobs working for the faculty. He became the first man to create a steam engine that was powerful enough to run a warship but was unable to patent the invention because he was a slave.

Another famous slave from Boston was named Onesimus. "He was presented to the minister Cotton Mather by his congregation as a gift, which is, of course, extremely troubling," Brown University history professor Ted Widmer told WGHB. "Cotton Mather was a true puritan. A towering, if controversial, figure, especially following the Salem witch hysteria to which his preaching and writings greatly contributed."

"Cotton Mather was interested in his slave whom he called Onesimus, the name of a slave belonging to St. Paul in the Bible," explained Widmer. Described by Mather as a 'pretty intelligent fellow,' Onesimus had a small scar on his arm, which he explained to Mather was why he had no fear of the era's single deadliest disease: smallpox. "Mather was fascinated by what Onesimus knew of inoculation practices back in Africa where he was from," said Widmer.

Viewed mainly with suspicion by the few Europeans of the era who were even aware of inoculation, the benefits of receiving inoculations were known at the time in places in places like China, Turkey, and West Africa.

"Our way of thinking of the world is often not accurate," said Widmer. "For centuries Europe was behind other parts of the world in its medical practices."

Although inoculation was common in certain parts of the world by the early 18th century, it was only just beginning to be discussed in England and colonial America at that time.

Bostonians like Mather were no strangers to smallpox. Outbreaks in 1690 and 1702 had devastated the colonial city. And Widmer says Mather took a keen interest in Onesimus' understanding of how the inoculation was done.

"They would take a small amount of a similar disease, sometimes cowpox, and they would open a cut and put a little drop of the disease into the bloodstream," explained Widmer. "And they knew that that was a way of developing resistance to it."

A Harvard University report further cemented what Onesimus accomplished after a smallpox outbreak once again gripped Boston in 1721. Mather campaigned for the systematic application of inoculations.

"Mather is largely credited with introducing inoculation to the colonies and doing a great deal to promote the use of this method as standard for smallpox prevention during the 1721 epidemic," Harvard authors wrote.

Then, they noted: "Mather is believed to have first learned about inoculation from his West African slave Onesimus, writing, 'he told me that he had undergone the operation which had given something of the small-pox and would forever preserve him from it, adding that was often used in West Africa.'

What followed was a fierce public debate, but also became one of the first widespread and well-documented uses of inoculation to combat an epidemic in the West.

Some people who got inoculated did die. Roughly one in 40 did, but roughly one in seven members of the general population dies, "so you had a much worse chance of surviving smallpox if you did nothing," according to WGHB's research.

Mather and Boylston both wrote about their findings, which were circulated at home and impressed the scientific elite in London, adding invaluable data at a crucial time that helped lay the groundwork for Edward Jenner's famed first smallpox vaccine 75 years later.

"Even though most of the city was on the wrong side and didn't want inoculation to happen they were smart enough to realize afterward that they had been wrong," Widmer said. "And so, there was a higher level of respect for science going forward."

The scourge of slavery would continue in Massachusetts for another 60 years, but as for the man whose knowledge sparked the breakthrough, Widmer said "Onesimus was recognized as the savior of a lot of Bostonians and was admired and then was emancipated, Onesimus was a hero. He gave of his knowledge freely and was himself freed."

Thomas, who has worked as an editor in medical and academic publishing for more than 25 years, added that it's important for African Americans to understand that immunizations were originally an African practice that Africans brought with them to America.

"Since then, African Americans played an important role in making vaccines safer and more effective," she said, noting that an African American woman scientist named Loney Gordon played a key role in the development of the vaccine against whooping cough (pertussis).

Enslaved African Americans' contributions to American innovation weren't limited to Onesimus. Enslaved African Americans, Henry Boyd,

Benjamin Bradley, Lewis Latimer, and Sarah E. Goode also left an indelible mark on American society through their resourcefulness, creativity, and determination.

Recognizing their achievements not only honors their legacy but also underscores the importance of acknowledging the often-overlooked inventors of our past. Their stories serve as a powerful reminder that innovation knows no bounds, transcending the shackles of bondage to shape history.

Henry Boyd, a skilled carpenter and cabinetmaker, was born into slavery in Kentucky in 1802. He developed an innovative method for constructing sturdy, durable bed frames known as the Boyd Bedstead. His design was so successful that it was widely replicated, marking a significant contribution to the American furniture industry.

Benjamin Bradley, born into slavery in 1830, demonstrated a remarkable aptitude in mechanical engineering. While working in a Washington, D.C. factory, he used his skills to construct a functioning steam-powered engine for a warship, the S.S. *Rappahannock*, during the Civil War. Bradley's innovation significantly advanced maritime technology.

Born in Chelsea, Massachusetts 1848, Lewis Latimer was an enslaved African American and an unsung hero in electrical engineering who would go on to revolutionize the field of electrical engineering.

Latimer's early exposure to innovation came through his father, George Latimer, a fugitive slave who settled in Massachusetts. George Latimer's escape from bondage and subsequent work as a janitor in the Massachusetts State House imbued Lewis with a deep appreciation for education and self-improvement.

Lewis Latimer's early aptitude for drawing and drafting led him to secure a position at a patent law firm, Crosby and Gould, in Boston. Here, under the mentorship of William S. Brown, Latimer honed his skills in technical illustration and gained a profound understanding of electrical inventions.

Latimer's most renowned achievement came in 1881 when he patented a method for producing a more durable carbon filament for incandescent lightbulbs. Before Latimer's innovation, the filaments used were made of materials that burned out quickly. His invention revolutionized the lighting industry, making electric lighting more practical and accessible to the masses.

Some of the greatest inventors of his time were vying for Latimer's talents. He worked closely with Alexander Graham Bell, assisting in drafting the patent for the telephone. Impressed by Latimer's expertise, Thomas Edison recruited him to work as a draftsman at the Edison Electric Light Company.

His contributions to Edison's company were invaluable, as Latimer played a pivotal role in developing the technology behind the incandescent lightbulb. His innovations significantly extended the lifespan and efficiency of this revolutionary invention.

Latimer's impact on the field of electrical engineering endures. His legacy extends beyond his own inventions, as he paved the way for future generations of inventors and engineers. Latimer's dedication to education and his passion for innovation continue to inspire those pursuing scientific discovery.

Efforts to recognize Latimer's achievements and ensure his place in the annals of history are underway, with initiatives to highlight his legacy in educational curricula and public awareness campaigns.

Latimer's story serves as a beacon of inspiration, a testament to the power of perseverance and intellectual curiosity. His innovations in electrical engineering continue to light the way for future generations of inventors. As the world increasingly acknowledges his invaluable contributions, Lewis Latimer's name rightfully takes its place among the giants of American innovation.

Benjamin Bradley, a remarkable figure born into bondage in 1830, stands as a testament to the power of ingenuity in the face of adversity. His contributions to American innovation, particularly in maritime technology, continue to inspire generations.

Like Latimer and others, Bradley's life began in the crucible of slavery, yet his aptitude for engineering and mechanical innovation would elevate him beyond the confines of his circumstances. While enslaved in a Washington, D.C. factory, Bradley honed his skills, displaying an exceptional talent for working with machinery.

Bradley's remarkable abilities would take center stage during the American Civil War. In 1862, he was tasked with an ambitious project: constructing a steam engine for the warship S.S. *Rappahannock*. Bradley's innovation propelled the vessel into the ranks of modern maritime technology, showcasing the potential of steam power for naval purposes.

Bradley's accomplishments were a beacon of hope for those who toiled under the yoke of slavery. His achievements not only improved the capabilities of the Union Navy but also shattered preconceived notions about the intellectual capabilities of enslaved individuals.

Bradley's impact extends beyond his groundbreaking work on the S.S. *Rappahannock*. His ingenuity and determination serve as a reminder of the untapped potential that existed within enslaved communities across America.

While Bradley's contributions have gained recognition in recent years, there is a growing call to elevate his legacy further. Initiatives to incorporate his story into educational curricula and public awareness campaigns are underway, ensuring that Bradley's name takes its rightful place in the pantheon of American innovators.

Bradley's story is another one of triumph over adversity, a testament to the power of human potential. His contributions to maritime technology remind us that innovation knows no bounds. As the world increasingly acknowledges his invaluable legacy, Bradley's name rightfully shines among the stars of American ingenuity.

Henry Boyd was born into slavery in 1802, Henry Boyd also left an indelible mark on American craftsmanship through his pioneering contributions to the furniture industry. His innovative designs and unwavering dedication to his craft also continue to inspire artisans and enthusiasts alike.

Boyd learned the art of woodworking as a young, enslaved man. His innate talent for carpentry quickly set him apart, showcasing an uncanny ability to transform raw materials into exquisite pieces of furniture.

In the mid-19th century, Boyd unveiled his most iconic creation—the Boyd Bedstead. The innovative piece of furniture revolutionized the industry with its sturdy construction and functional design. Boyd's bed frame quickly gained popularity, becoming a staple in households across America.

Boyd's contributions were not confined to the workshop. His craftsmanship stood as a testament to the ingenuity and skill of enslaved artisans, challenging prevailing notions about their creative capabilities. The Boyd Bedstead symbolized excellence in woodworking, reflecting Boyd's dedication to his craft.

Henry Boyd's impact on the American furniture industry endures, even in 2024. His innovative designs and commitment to quality craftsmanship set a standard of excellence that inspires artisans and woodworkers today.

While Boyd's contributions were often overlooked in his time, there is a growing movement to honor his legacy. Initiatives to incorporate his story into educational curricula and public awareness campaigns aim to ensure that Henry Boyd's name takes its rightful place among the pioneers of American craftsmanship. His contributions to the furniture industry serve as a reminder that innovation knows no bounds.

Sarah E. Goode, another often unsung hero of American innovation, made a profound mark on history with her groundbreaking contributions to furniture design. Born in 1855, Goode's entrepreneurial spirit and inventive mind continue to inspire generations of innovators.

Goode's journey began in slavery, but her determination and vision would lead her to become a pioneer in American business. After gaining her freedom, Goode settled in Chicago, a city bustling with opportunities and a burgeoning market for innovation.

In 1885, Goode secured a patent for her most significant invention, the convertible cabinet bed. This innovative piece of furniture she designed addressed a pressing need in small urban settings where space was at a premium. By day, it functioned as an elegant cabinet, and by night, it transformed into a comfortable bed, providing a practical solution for small living spaces. Goode's invention was a testament to her ingenuity and a pioneering achievement for women and African Americans in business. Her success challenged societal norms, breaking barriers for future generations of entrepreneurs.

The convertible cabinet bed revolutionized home furniture for urban living, particularly in fast-growing cities like Chicago. Goode's invention addressed a pressing need for space-saving solutions, setting a new standard for functional and versatile furniture.

Goode's contributions have recently gained wide recognition, and there is a growing movement to honor her legacy more widely. Initiatives to incorporate her story into educational curricula and public awareness campaigns aim to ensure that Goode's name rightfully takes its place among the trailblazers of American entrepreneurship.

Like other enslaved inventors, Goode's story is one of resilience, vision, and a testament to the limitless possibilities of human innovation and serve as a reminder that groundbreaking ideas can emerge from unexpected sources.

CHAPTER 12

Environmental Racism, Another Legacy of the Transatlantic Slave Trade

"Environmental protection doesn't happen in a vacuum. One can't separate the impact on the environment from the impact on our families and communities."
— South Carolina Representative JIM CLYBURN

"Climate crisis and social injustice are inextricably linked. Our economic system must work not only for the few, but for all nations and all people, especially communities that are impacted first and worst by the climate crisis. We demand not only action, but transparency and accountability from governments on existing commitments. Now is the time for change and now is the time for real action."
— JEROME FOSTER II,
the youngest-ever White House advisor for environmental justice

"Environmental racism" was a term coined in 1982 by Dr. Benjamin F. Chavis, Jr., to describe the systemic environmental injustices committed against marginalized communities, particularly those of African descent. He stated that "There are four factors lead to environmental racism: lack of affordable land, lack of political power, lack of mobility, and the presence of poverty."

Cheap land is sought by corporations and governmental bodies. As a result, communities which cannot effectively resist these corporations and governmental bodies and cannot access political power cannot negotiate just costs. Communities with minimized socioeconomic mobility cannot relocate. Lack of financial contributions also reduces the communities' ability to act both physically and politically.*

---

* Colquette, Kelly Michele; Robertson, Elizabeth A. Henry (1991). "Environmental Racism: The Causes, Consequences, and Commendations." *Tulane Environmental Law Journal.* 5 (1): 153–207.

Dr. Chavis defined environmental racism in five categories: "racial discrimination in defining environmental policies, discriminatory enforcement of regulations and laws, deliberate targeting of minority communities as hazardous waste dumping sites, official sanctioning of dangerous pollutants in minority communities, and the exclusion of people of color from environmental leadership positions."

The Transatlantic Slave Trade, spanning over five centuries, is arguably human history's most profound and enduring tragedy. Its legacy has deeply permeated various aspects of contemporary society, leaving an indelible mark on the affected regions' socio-political, economic, and environmental landscapes.

The legacy manifests itself in multifaceted ways, notably through the lens of environmental racism, the fight for reparations, and the enduring consequences that continue to reverberate across the globe.

Rooted in historical patterns of exploitation, transatlantic slave trade set in motion a trajectory of environmental inequality that persists to this day. Enslaved Africans were subjected to inhumane conditions and forced to toil on plantations and in mines, often in ecologically precarious environments. This exploitation led to the degradation of local ecosystems and laid the foundation for enduring socio-environmental disparities.

Environmental racism is an insidious form of discrimination that disproportionately impacts marginalized communities, particularly those of color. The practice involves deliberately placing ecological hazards, such as toxic waste sites, landfills, and polluting industries, in areas predominantly inhabited by minority populations. The African American community has primarily been the most affected. The wide-ranging effects of environmental racism encompass health disparities, economic inequities, social injustice, and a diminished quality of life. Through compelling case studies, this chapter aims to shed light on the pervasive and enduring consequences of this deeply rooted issue.

One of the most palpable consequences of environmental racism is its adverse impact on public health. Communities subjected to environmental injustice often face higher rates of respiratory illnesses, cancers, and other health complications. For instance, in Flint, Michigan, a predominantly African American community, lead-contaminated drinking water resulted in a public health crisis. The exposure to lead led to neurological damage in children, underscoring how environmental racism exacerbates existing health disparities.

Environmental racism also contributes to economic disparities, as marginalized communities are often deprived of economic opportunities. Industries that pose significant environmental risks tend to concentrate in these areas, offering limited job prospects with inadequate wages. A stark example of petrochemical plants surrounding predominantly African American communities is the Cancer Alley region of Louisiana. Despite these industries' economic activity, residents struggle with high rates of poverty and limited access to good jobs.

Communities affected by environmental racism often face disenfranchisement and limited access to resources. This is evident in the struggle for clean and safe living environments. For instance, in Warren County, North Carolina, a predominantly African American community was the setting of a hazardous waste landfill in the 1980s that led to widespread protests. Despite this opposition, the landfill was established, highlighting the systemic disregard for the voices and concerns of marginalized communities.

In 2022, for the better part of a month, Dr. Chavis Jr. traveled back and forth to North Carolina from Washington, D.C. to help spearhead plans and events to observe the 40th anniversary of the Warren County protests.

In 1982 other protests occurred after officials dumped polychlorinated biphenyls (PCBs) in predominately Black communities.

On Saturday, September 24, 2022, Dr. Chavis welcomed U.S. Environmental Protection Agency Administrator Michael Regan, formally introducing him as he announced the establishment of a new national office charged with advancing environmental justice and civil rights.

Creating the new Office of Environmental Justice and External Civil Rights delivers on President Biden's commitment to "elevate these critical issues to the highest levels of the government and solidifies the agency's commitment to delivering justice and equity for all," EPA officials stated.

Chavis introduced Regan to a large crowd in Warrenton that included local and national media and championed the administrator's hiring.

"When I first coined the term environmental racism, our communities were being deliberately targeted for toxic waste and hazardous materials," Dr. Chavis informed an enthusiastic crowd gathered in his home state.

"I'm so happy that the administration had the good sense to put a brother over the EPA," he continued. "This brother not only represents historically Black colleges and universities but also the community—a community in Wayne County with a history like Warren County of standing up for justice. Thank God we have a freedom fighter at the EPA. Thank God Michael Regan is the administrator of the EPA at a time when we connect civil rights with environmental justice and will have solutions."

Regan said the new office plans to dedicate more than 200 EPA staff members across ten regions.

The administrator asserted that their mission is to solve environmental challenges in underserved communities that have been occurring for far too long. Staffers would engage with communities about environmental justice concerns to understand their needs and tribal, state, and local partners.

The staff would also manage and disburse "historic levels of grants and technical assistance; work with other EPA offices to incorporate environmental justice into the agency's programs, policies, and processes, as allowed by law; and ensure EPA funding recipients comply with applicable civil rights laws," Regan promised.

He also announced that the Biden-Harris administration would seek Senate confirmation of an assistant administrator to lead the new office.

"President Biden and I have been clear: we must ground our work to address the climate crisis and our greatest environmental challenges in justice and equity," said Vice President Kamala Harris. "The establishment of a new office dedicated to advancing environmental justice and civil rights at EPA will ensure the lived experiences of underserved communities are central to our decision-making while supporting community-driven solutions."

From day one, Regan said Biden and the EPA had been committed to improving environmental justice and civil rights, "Ensuring that underserved and overburdened communities are at the forefront of our work," Regan insisted.

"With the launch of a new national program office, we are embedding environmental justice and civil rights into the DNA of EPA and ensuring that people who've struggled to address their concerns see action to solve the problems they've been facing for generations."

The Inflation Reduction Act's historic $60 billion investment in environmental justice is a critical component of the new office's responsibility for implementing and delivering a $3 billion climate and environmental justice block grant program.

The office also will ensure EPA's implementation of other funding programs provided by the Inflation Reduction Act, Bipartisan Infrastructure Law, and regular appropriations meet or exceed the President's Justice40 Initiative.

Administration officials said the new office counted as the latest significant action under Biden's aggressive approach to embedding environmental justice, civil rights, and equity across the government. It follows the launch of several initiatives designed to address the impacts of those living in underserved communities overburdened by pollution.

Initiatives include the establishment of the first-ever White House Environmental Justice Advisory Council (WHEJAC); the launch of the Justice40 Initiative, which aims to provide 40 percent of the overall benefits of federal investments relating to climate change, clean energy, and related areas to disadvantaged communities; and more than 200 policy actions to move Biden's ambitious environmental justice and civil rights agenda forward.

The EPA created the Office of Environmental Justice and External Civil Rights Office by merging three existing programs at the agency: the Office of Environmental Justice, the External Civil Rights Compliance Office, and the Conflict Prevention and Resolution Center.

Officials said the new office would:

- ⊙ Improve and enhance the agency's ability to infuse equity, civil rights, and environmental justice principles and priorities into all EPA practices, policies, and programs.

- ⊙ Support the fair treatment and meaningful involvement of all people concerning the development, implementation, and enforcement of environmental laws, regulations, and policies regardless of race, color, national origin, or income.

⊚ Engage communities with environmental justice concerns and increase support for community-led action through grants and technical assistance.

⊚ Enforce federal civil rights laws that prohibit discrimination based on race, color, or national origin (including limited-English proficiency), sex; disability; or age by applicants for and recipients of federal financial assistance from EPA.

⊚ Provide services and expertise in alternative dispute resolution, environmental conflict resolution, consensus-building, and collaborative problem-solving.

"This is a historic day. Not just for Warren County, North Carolina, where the environmental justice movement began, but for the millions of Americans across this country who have been demanding and fighting tirelessly for environmental justice for decades," North Carolina Democratic Rep. G.K. Butterfield stated.

He added: "I commend President Biden, Vice President Harris, and EPA Administrator Michael Regan on their work to create the Office of Environmental Justice and External Civil Rights. "Today's announcement, which comes on the heels of the historic climate and environmental justice investments in the Inflation Reduction Act, is another bold example that the Biden-Harris Administration and Congress will ensure every community has a voice and the investments needed to grow and thrive."

Butterfield concluded his speech by saying, "Working together, we will solve the climate crisis and make America's clean energy economy the envy of the world."

Dr. Chavis had repeatedly noted that environmental racism could also profoundly impact educational opportunities. Schools in areas burdened by ecological hazards often face challenges in providing a conducive learning environment. For example, in South Bronx in New York, in a predominantly Hispanic community, high asthma rates resulting from air pollution exacerbate absenteeism and hinder educational attainment. This exemplifies how environmental racism extends its reach to the realm of education, perpetuating cycles of inequality.

Housing discrimination is another facet of environmental racism. Minority communities are frequently subjected to substandard housing conditions, with limited access to affordable and safe housing. The situation in West Dallas, Texas, where a community with a large African American population faced the threat of eviction due to plans for a new industrial development, is an example. The proposed project disregarded the residents' right to safe and secure housing, underscoring the systemic nature of this issue.

The wide-ranging effects of environmental racism are pervasive and deeply ingrained in the fabric of society. From health disparities and economic inequities to social injustice and housing discrimination, marginalized communities bear the brunt of environmental injustice. Through case studies, we gain insight into the lived experiences of these communities, shedding light on the urgent need for systemic change. Vigilant activists like Dr. Chavis have said we must recognize and address the enduring consequences of environmental racism to create a more equitable and just future for all.

The repercussions of this historical exploitation are starkly evident in regions with a history of slavery, such as Brazil and the Caribbean. The socio-environmental consequences are palpable in Brazil, a nation that received the highest number of enslaved Africans during the trade. Afro-Brazilian communities often find themselves disproportionately located in areas afflicted by environmental hazards, from polluted water sources to proximity to toxic waste sites. These communities face heightened vulnerability to the impacts of climate change, perpetuating a cycle of environmental injustice that harks back to the days of slavery.

Similarly, in the Caribbean, the systemic legacy of the Transatlantic Slave Trade reverberates through the present-day environmental landscape. Many Afro-Caribbean communities are in vulnerable areas to natural disasters, which climate change has made worse. The inadequate response and resource allocation from governments further compound the vulnerability of these communities. This pattern exemplifies the enduring nature of environmental racism, firmly rooted in enslaved Africans' historical exploitation and disenfranchisement.

The call for reparations, seeking redress for the historical injustices of the Transatlantic Slave Trade, has gained momentum in recent decades. Advocates argue that the systemic legacy of slavery persists in contemporary socio-economic disparities, and reparations are a crucial step towards addressing these inequities. Various initiatives, from legislative proposals to grassroots movements, seek to rectify the enduring consequences of historical injustice.

England, a significant player in the Transatlantic Slave Trade, has grappled with its own legacy. The profits derived from the trade laid the foundation for much of the nation's economic prosperity. Today, the call for reparations gains traction as activists argue that this accumulated wealth is intimately tied to the systemic inequalities that persist within the country. The demand for reparations resonates not only in England but across former colonial territories where the echoes of slavery's legacy remain palpable.

Indeed, the systemic legacy of the Transatlantic Slave Trade is a tapestry woven with threads of environmental racism, the fight for reparations, and ongoing socio-environmental consequences. From Brazil and the Caribbean to England and beyond, the enduring ramifications of this dark chapter in history continue to shape contemporary society.

An October 2023 report from the Sentencing Project has revealed significant strides have been made in reducing racial inequities in incarceration over the past two decades. However, the study also warns that ongoing pushback from policymakers threatens to impede further progress.

The report, titled "One in Five: Ending Racial Inequity in Incarceration," highlights a notable decline in the lifetime likelihood of imprisonment for Black men born in 2001 compared to those born in 1981. While one in three Black men born in 1981 faced the prospect of imprisonment, the figure has now dropped to one in five for those born in 2001.

The authors attribute the decline to reforms, particularly in drug law enforcement and sentencing for drug and property offenses. Urban areas, predominantly home to communities of color, have significantly reduced imprisonment rates.

Despite these positive trends, the report underscores that imprisonment levels remain alarmingly high nationwide, particularly for Black Americans. The authors caution that the U.S. remains entrenched in the era of mass incarceration, with a 25 percent reduction in the total prison population since 2009, following a nearly 700 percent surge in imprisonment since 1972.

The report further notes that the prison population in 2021 was nearly six times larger than it was half a century ago, before the mass incarceration era, and continued to expand in 2022. The U.S. also maintains a five to eight times higher prison and jail incarceration rate than France, Canada, and Germany. Notably, states such as Arkansas, Louisiana, Mississippi, and Oklahoma have incarceration rates nearly 50 percent above the national average.

"The reluctance to fully correct sentencing excesses, particularly for violent crimes as supported by criminological evidence, prolongs the harm and futility of mass incarceration," the authors concluded, emphasizing that racial equity in incarceration remains an elusive goal.

The report also highlights persistent disparities among different racial and ethnic groups. The lifetime likelihood of imprisonment for Black men born in 2001, while reduced, remains four times that of their white counterparts. Black women face an imprisonment rate 1.6 times higher than white women in 2021.

The Sentencing Project stressed that addressing these disparities necessitates a dual approach, targeting the criminal legal system and the underlying socioeconomic conditions contributing to higher crime rates among people of color.

However, the momentum for continued progress remains precarious. Recent increases in specific crime categories, particularly homicides, during the COVID-19 pandemic and the opioid overdose crisis have prompted lawmakers to reevaluate criminal justice reforms. This has resulted in a bipartisan backlash, including proposals to expand mandatory minimum sentences for federal drug offenses.

The Sentencing Project said it's taking proactive measures to safeguard and build on the progress achieved thus far. They are producing four reports that delve into the persistence of racial injustice in the criminal legal system while highlighting promising reforms. The first installment provides an overview of prison and jail incarceration trends and community supervision, with subsequent reports focusing on police interactions, crime rates, and critical drivers of disparity within the criminal legal system. "These reports aim to contribute to ongoing efforts to achieve a more equitable and just criminal justice system for all Americans," the authors wrote.

Despite recent changes that have decreased the number of people involved in the criminal justice system and have addressed racial and ethnic disparities, "we are still in a time where mass incarceration is a major issue," the authors continued. They affirmed that excessive control and punishment, especially targeting people of color, do not help achieve community safety goals and harm families and communities. While people of color face higher crime rates than whites, they tend to be less supportive of stringent crime control measures when compared to whites, the authors asserted.

To address the injustices outlined in this report, the authors said there remains a need for policies and practices changes that unfairly affect communities of color, and authorities should seek to reduce excessive punishment for all individuals. "The United States would still have an incarceration crisis," University of Pennsylvania professor Marie Gottschalk wrote in the report, "even if it were locking up African Americans at 'only' the rate at which whites in the United States are currently incarcerated—or if it were not locking up any African Americans at all."

CHAPTER THIRTEEN

The Myth of Black-on-Black Crime

"White-on-white crime is a devastation in America like so-called Black-on-Black crime. It's not Black or white-on-white crime. It is proximity to murder."
—MICHAEL ERIC DYSON, scholar

"Black-on Black crime is jargon, violence on language, which vanishes the men who engineered the covenants, who fixed the loans, who planned the projects, who built the streets and sold red ink by the barrel."

—TA-NEHISI COATES, author

The narrative of Black-on-Black crime, pushed through the consciousness of America since the end of slavery, has not only perpetuated harmful stereotypes but has also had profound and far-reaching consequences for the African American community. This narrative, deeply rooted in historical injustices, has been used to oppress Black people further, often deflecting attention from systemic issues.

To comprehend the full extent of the impact of the Black-on-Black crime narrative, one must first acknowledge the historical context in which it emerged. Slavery, Jim Crow, and systemic racism have systematically disadvantaged African Americans for centuries. These structural inequalities, rooted in a legacy of discrimination, continue to influence socioeconomic conditions within African American communities.

According to the U.S. Census Bureau, in 2020, the poverty rate for Black individuals was 18.8 percent, compared to 7.3 percent for white individuals. This economic inequality is closely linked to crime rates, as studies consistently show a correlation between poverty and criminal activity.

Access to quality education is also a crucial factor in breaking cycles of poverty and crime. However, African American students face systemic disadvantages, including underfunded schools, lower teacher to student ratios, and limited access to advanced coursework. According to the National Center for Education Statistics, in 2018–2019, only 20 percent of African American students scored proficient or above in 8th-grade reading, compared to 45 percent of white students.

Discrimination in the job market because they lack opportunities to receive a higher education further exacerbates economic disparities.

African American students have less access to college-ready courses than white students, according to the United Negro College Fund. In fact, in 2011-12, only 57 percent of black students had access to a full range of math and science courses necessary for college readiness, compared to 81 percent of Asian American students and 71 percent of white students. Even when black students do have access to honors or advanced placement courses, they are vastly underrepresented in these courses. Black and Latino students represent 38 percent of students in schools that offer AP courses. Still, only 29 percent of students enrolled in at least one AP course, the United Negro College Fund reported.

The organization noted that Black and Latino students also have less access to gifted and talented education programs than white students. African American students are often located in schools with less qualified teachers, teachers with lower salaries, and novice teachers. Research indicates that teacher expectations for African American students may be biased, and non-black teachers tend to have lower expectations for black students than black teachers. African American students are less likely to be college-ready. Sixty-one percent of black students who took the ACT in 2015 did not meet any of the four ACT college readiness benchmarks. This is almost double the rate of all students, which is 31 percent.

Due to discipline problems, black students spend less time in the classroom, which further hinders their access to a high quality education. Black students are nearly two times as likely to be suspended without educational services as white students. Black students are also 3.8 times as likely to receive one or more out-of-school suspensions as white students. Black children comprise 19 percent of preschoolers in the country, but they account for 47 percent of those receiving multiple out-of-school suspensions.

In comparison, white students represent 41 percent of preschool enrollment but only 28 percent of those receiving more than one out-of-school suspension. Even more troubling, black students are 2.3 times more likely to receive a referral to law enforcement or be subject to a school-related arrest than white students. Students of color are often concentrated in schools with fewer resources. Schools with 90 percent or more students of color spend $733 less per student per year than schools with 90 percent or more white students.

According to the Office for Civil Rights, 1.6 million students attend a school with a sworn law enforcement officer (SLEO), but not a school counselor. In fact, the national student-to-counselor ratio is 491 to 1; however, the American School Counselor Association recommends a ratio of 250 to 1. In 2015, the average reading score for white students on the National Assessment of Educational Progress (NAEP) 4th and 8th-grade exam was 26 points higher than Black students. Similar gaps are apparent in math. The 12th-grade assessment also shows alarming disparities, with only seven percent of black students performing at or above proficient on the math exam in 2015, compared to 32 percent of white students. There is an evident lack of Black representation in school personnel.

According to a 2016 Department of Education report, in 2011–12, only 10 percent of public school principals were Black, compared to 80 percent white. Eighty-two percent of public school educators are white, compared to 18 percent of teachers of color. In addition, Black male teachers only constitute two percent of the teaching workforce. Most recently, in 2023, USAFacts.org found that about 15 percent of K-12 public school students are Black, but they make up more than 30 percent of students who are suspended, expelled, or arrested. The racial disparity exists for public preschool students as well. Black preschoolers are 18 percent of enrolled students but 43 percent of out-of-school suspensions.

Additionally, studies repeatedly show that African Americans face higher unemployment rates and are often paid less than their white counterparts for equivalent work. This economic disenfranchisement can lead to increased crime rates in disadvantaged communities.

Inequality in modern-day unemployment rates has received considerable attention, including work demonstrating that Black teens, Black women, and Black men's unemployment in the United States are consistently worse than that of white teens, white women, and white men. Using historical data from the Bureau of Labor Statistics (BLS), this post sheds light on longer-term inequality trends, looking back over six decades.

Readily available data from the BLS shows that unemployment rates for Black men and women have been roughly double those for white men and women, respectively, since 1972. These data also show that the unemployment rate for Black men has exceeded that for Black women since 1980 (except for 1987 and 1998). This post reports on unpublished BLS data, demonstrating that the stark inequality in unemployment rates is longstanding: non-white people have had unemployment rates more than double those of white people as far back as 1954. On the other hand, the patterns in unemployment rates for Black women relative to Black men have shifted over time.

In 1972, the Bureau of Labor Statistics (BLS) started to report the unemployment rate separately by sex for Black people, making it possible to assess trends for Black women and men individually. Before 1972, BLS collected this data in two broad racial categories: white and non-white, referred to as "Black and other."

Writing for the Brookings Institute, Tina Ford said she began by making clear who "Black and other" likely were in the historic BLS data. Black people comprised at least 90% of the non-white population from 1950 to 1970. Thus, previously unreported BLS data for "Black and other" people could be used to make inferences about Black people's unemployment experience from 1954 to 1971, Ford wrote. In 1954, the unemployment rate for non-white men was more than double white men; the unemployment rate for non-white women compared to white women was nearly double.

Non-white women experienced a higher unemployment rate relative to non-white men from 1962 to 1979, with the most significant gap in 1967 of a 3.1 percentage point difference. That was a distinct change from more recent unemployment trends for Black people. Except for 1987 and 1998, the unemployment rate for Black women was lower than the rate for Black men from 1980 to 2021. The most considerable divergence between unemployment rates for Black men and women can be seen in 2009–2011, where Black men's unemployment reached as high as 18.4 percent in 2010 (4.6 percentage points higher than Black women in that year), while Black women's unemployment peaked at 14.1percent in 2011 (3.7 percentage points lower than Black men in that year).

Neither of these more recent peaks reflects the height of Black unemployment in the U.S. In 1983, Black women saw an 18.6 percent unemployment rate: Black men 20.3 percent. These unemployment rates were more than 2.3 times those of white women and men in 1983. While Black and white unemployment fell in the years following 1983, the Black-white unemployment gap did not. Indeed, Black men experienced unemployment rates 2.6 times those of white men in 1989; Black women had 2.4 times the unemployment rate of white women.

The lowest unemployment rate for Black people in the U.S. can be seen in 2019, with Black men at 6.6 percent and Black women at 5 percent. Even then, however, unemployment rates for Black men and women were roughly two times those of their white counterparts. "These data demonstrate that the trend of Black unemployment being double that of white unemployment has endured since 1954 and remains so, even as national unemployment rates fall," Ford concluded.

All of these disparities lend itself to an increased crime rate. Additionally, the media plays an influential role in shaping public perception and understanding of social issues. The overemphasis on crime within African American communities and underreporting or misrepresentation of crime in predominantly white communities perpetuates harmful stereotypes. A study published in the journal *Race and Justice* found that media outlets tend to disproportionately report crimes committed by Black individuals, further reinforcing racial biases.

The narrative of Black-on-Black crime is often used to divert attention away from systemic issues and perpetuate racial stereotypes. It is crucial to acknowledge that intra-racial crime is not unique to the African

American community; it occurs in all racial and ethnic groups. However, the disproportionate focus on Black-on-Black crime reinforces the false notion that crime within African American communities is somehow inherent to their culture.

Quite simply, most crimes white individuals commit occur within predominantly white communities. This is a statistical reality in any racially homogeneous society. However, it is rarely framed as a racially specific issue, as it should not be. To solely attribute crime to race oversimplifies the problem because it is a complex socioeconomic phenomenon that depends on various factors.

Similarly, crime within Asian communities is primarily intra-racial, occurring among individuals of Asian descent. However, discussions surrounding Asian-on-Asian crime are conspicuously absent from public discourse. This absence highlights the selective nature of the narrative surrounding crime, further emphasizing the need for a more nuanced understanding.

To combat the harmful impact of the Black-on-Black crime narrative, fostering a more inclusive and nuanced dialogue about crime in America is imperative. This must involve addressing the systemic issues contributing to crime rates within disadvantaged communities, such as poverty, lack of access to quality education, and discrimination in the job market.

There's little doubt that the narrative of Black-on-Black crime has had a profound and detrimental impact on the African American community. By understanding the historical context and examining the socioeconomic disparities contributing to crime rates, we can dismantle harmful stereotypes. It is essential to shift the narrative towards a more inclusive and empathetic understanding of the complex factors contributing to crime, ultimately working towards a more just and equitable society for all communities, regardless of race.

CHAPTER FOURTEEN

The Deepening Wealth Gap: Decades of Policy Failures Leave Formerly Enslaved People Behind

"Oh America, how often have you taken necessities from the masses to give luxuries to the classes ... God never intended for one group of people to live in superfluous inordinate wealth, while others live in abject deadening poverty."

—DR. MARTIN LUTHER KING, JR.
American Civil Rights Leader, November 4, 1956

*I*n the tapestry of American society, the wealth gap remains a glaring and persistent stain. Nowhere is this divide more pronounced than among African Americans, who continue to grapple with systemic barriers rooted in a history of discriminatory policies at various levels of government. From municipal ordinances to federal laws, these policies have left a profound and enduring impact on the financial well-being of African American communities.

The roots of this wealth disparity trace back to slavery, which forcibly denied African Americans the opportunity to accumulate wealth or property. After Emancipation, the promise of "40 acres and a mule" was never realized, leaving newly freed individuals without the means to build economic security. The emergence of discriminatory policies further exacerbated this systemic disadvantage.

At the municipal level, redlining is one of the most notorious policies perpetuating the wealth gap. In the mid-20th century, the Federal Housing Administration (FHA) systematically denied loans to African American communities, effectively confining them to segregated, underinvested neighborhoods. This practice deprived families of homeownership, a cornerstone of wealth accumulation, and stifled economic development in these areas.

Moreover, discriminatory zoning practices and housing covenants further segregated communities, limiting access to quality education, healthcare, and employment opportunities. The ripple effects of these policies are still felt today, as neighborhoods created under these circumstances continue to face economic challenges.

Throughout the 20th century, urban centers across the country witnessed a cycle of disinvestment in predominantly African American neighborhoods. Essential services, such as quality education, healthcare, and public infrastructure, were consistently underfunded, leaving residents at a distinct disadvantage. These patterns of neglect have persisted over the decades, contributing to African Americans' erosion of economic opportunity.

Efforts to reverse this trend have needed to be more consistent, with some cities now implementing targeted reinvestment programs. However, the legacy of disinvestment remains a significant barrier to economic progress, necessitating sustained, community-driven initiatives to revitalize neglected areas.

Federal policies in recent decades, such as the "War on Drugs," disproportionately targeted African American communities. The resulting mass incarceration shattered families and communities and severely hindered economic mobility. Upon release, formerly incarcerated individuals face a daunting array of barriers to employment and housing, perpetuating cycles of poverty.

The collateral consequences of these policies extend far beyond prison walls. Limited access to job opportunities and the stigma of a criminal record creates formidable challenges for reentry into society. Efforts to reform sentencing laws and implement reintegration programs are essential steps toward breaking this cycle of disadvantage.

Federal policies designed to address housing disparities paradoxically exacerbate the wealth gap. While the Fair Housing Act of 1968 aimed to combat discrimination, its enforcement was often lax, allowing discriminatory practices to persist. Additionally, underfunding and insufficient oversight plagued affordable housing programs, limiting their impact on African American communities.

Efforts to rectify these issues are underway, with calls for increased funding and strengthened enforcement of fair housing laws. Additionally, innovative approaches to affordable housing, such as community land trusts and inclusionary zoning, show promise for providing stable, affordable housing options for African American families.

Access to capital and resources has long been a hurdle for African American entrepreneurs. Financial discrimination and a lack of investment in minority-owned businesses have slowed the growth of companies in these areas, stopping families from building wealth that will last for generations.

Efforts to address this disparity include targeted investment in minority-owned businesses and initiatives to increase access to affordable loans and mentorship programs. Additionally, fostering an inclusive business environment through supplier diversity programs and equitable procurement practices can create opportunities for African American entrepreneurs to thrive.

Addressing the entrenched wealth gap requires a multi-faceted approach. Reforms at the federal, state, and municipal levels are imperative. This includes targeted education, healthcare, and infrastructure investments in historically neglected communities. Additionally, policies aimed at combating discrimination in housing, employment, and lending must be rigorously enforced.

Moreover, initiatives that foster economic empowerment, such as affordable housing programs, access to quality education, and support for minority-owned businesses, must be prioritized. By dismantling the policies that have historically hindered African American progress, we can begin to forge a more inclusive and equitable future.

In the face of this deepening wealth gap, acknowledging the historical injustices that created it is crucial. America, if she has the desire, can rectify these disparities, and build a more just and prosperous society for all Americans through concerted, sustained efforts.

In October 2023, the Black Press reported that the National Association of Real Estate Brokers (NAREB) launched a Building Black Wealth

Tour to give Black families and individuals the information they need to purchase homes, make wise investments, and engage in other activities to increase their wealth. Working with the African American Mayors Association and the National Bar Association, the Building Black Wealth Tour will visit more than 60 cities over the next two years as the collaboration organizes classes, workshops, and one-on-one counseling to advise families on homebuying, investing, and careers in real estate.

"We believe the time for action on Black wealth is now," said Dr. Courtney Johnson Rose, NAREB's president. "NAREB is urging our Black communities to take the journey towards wealth. Come to our events in your city and learn what you need to purchase a home. We are helping Black families overcome the biased public policies and private practices that created the vast wealth gap in America today." Asserting that the situation is "intolerable," Dr. Rose said that, on average, Black families own about 24 cents for every one dollar of white family wealth, according to the Federal Reserve. Homeownership, a critical component of Black wealth, has declined for Blacks nearly every quarter since the pandemic, leaving Blacks with the lowest homeownership percentage of any demographic in America.

Despite the contributions of the 1968 Fair Housing Act, 55 years later, the racial homeownership gap has widened. In 1960, 38 percent of Blacks owned homes, while white homeownership was 65 percent, a 27-point gap. In 2022, the rate of homeownership among whites was 74.4 percent compared to 45 percent for Blacks, a spread of 29.4 percent and the most extensive gap since 1890!

Homeownership is the driver of wealth, especially for Blacks. The equity from owning a home can be used to start a business, pay for a college education, and comfortably retire. It is the centerpiece of family economic security.

The first Building Black Wealth Tour event was held in Houston, and NAREB officials said it was a rousing success, with hundreds of participants. Each event includes festive youth activities and aims to empower Black communities with steps towards homeownership, property investment, starting a business, and other wealth-building opportunities.

Additionally, a workshop covered family-owned property that descendants of a deceased person whose estate did not pass probate jointly owned. The descendants, or heirs, have the right to use the property, but they need a clear or marketable title since the estate issues are unresolved. This has become a critical issue nationwide. Thus, the Black Wealth Tour educates Black consumers on properly passing along real estate and protecting themselves and the community from gentrification.

The NAREB State of Housing in Black America (SHIBA) report found more than two million mortgage-ready Black Americans nationwide. These families and individuals have the credit and income to qualify for a home mortgage. NAREB said they plan to find them. Over the next two years, NAREB promised to sponsor events nationwide.

The Black Press also reported that sixty years after the Rev. Dr. Martin Luther King Jr. delivered his iconic "I Have a Dream" speech during the March on Washington for Jobs and Freedom, a groundbreaking new report has laid bare the stark truth of ongoing Black economic inequality in the United States.

Titled "Still A Dream: Over 500 Years to Black Economic Equality," the report, co-authored by prominent experts Dedrick Asante-Muhammad, Chuck Collins, Omar Ocampo, and Sally Sim and published by the Institute for Policy Studies (IPS) and National Community Reinvestment Coalition (NCRC), underscores the enduring disparities faced by Black Americans and highlights the pressing need for concerted action to address these disparities.

"Sixty years ago, Dr. King observed that America has defaulted on this promissory note to Black citizens," stated Chuck Collins, an IPS senior scholar who directs the Program on Inequality and the Common Good in Washington, D.C.

"Six decades later, despite incremental progress on some fronts, the check of opportunity has still come back with insufficient funds."

Asante-Muhammad, chief of Race, Wealth, and Community for NCRC, lamented, "It is deeply troubling that, sixty years after the March on Washington for Jobs and Freedom, Black economic equality remains nothing more than a dream for most Black Americans."

"The revelation that it would take more than 500 additional years to close the economic gap for Black Americans is a stark reminder of the systemic inequities that persist," Asante-Muhammad asserted.

Sally Sim, a senior organizer and project specialist at NCRC, emphasized the situation's urgency. "The sobering projection and findings of our report sixty years after the March on Washington for Jobs and Freedom reinforce that the dream for economic equality for Black Americans remains unfulfilled," Sim stated.

"On this historic anniversary, let us turn this report into a catalyst for meaningful action towards comprehensive solutions and public support for policies and initiatives that promote black economic equality."

Some key findings from the comprehensive report were that, despite modest advancements made by African Americans since the 1960s, including reduced poverty rates, increased high school attainment, and lower unemployment rates, income disparities between Black and white Americans have only slightly improved.

The report exposes that in 2021, African Americans earn 62 cents to every dollar earned by white families. The report's authors said that, at this rate, achieving income parity would take an astonishing 513 years. Further, the wealth gap between Black and non-Black Americans has experienced only marginal growth, with African Americans possessing 18 cents for every dollar of non-Black wealth in 2019.

If this pace continues, it will take approximately 780 years for Black wealth to match non-Black wealth. Median household income for African Americans has shown minimal growth, growing just 0.36 percent since the turn of the century. Strikingly, it remained lower than white median family income in 1963. Even after over six decades, the Black-white home-ownership divide persists.

Black homeownership grew from 38 percent in 1960 to 44 percent in 2021, while white homeownership surged from 64 percent in 1960 to 74 percent in 2021.

The report outlined a series of recommendations to combat Black economic inequality:

1. Advocate for full employment and guaranteed jobs to ensure equal economic opportunities for all.

2. Enact a substantial land and homeownership program to address the enduring homeownership gap between Black and white Americans.

3. Commit to individual asset building, including financial education, asset matching programs, and supportive policies, to facilitate access to wealth-building opportunities for Black Americans.

4. Implement policies to reduce dynastic concentrations of wealth and power, tackling the structural barriers that impede economic progress for Black Americans.

5. Explore targeted reparations to address historical injustices and provide meaningful redress for Black Americans' economic disparities.

The authors noted that as the nation reflects on King's enduring vision for equality and justice, the report serves as a sobering reminder that pursuing Black economic equality remains an unmet challenge in America.

"The findings of this report are sobering and demand immediate and comprehensive action to address the economic disparities faced by African Americans," remarked Omar Ocampo, a researcher for the Program on Inequality and the Common Good at IPS. "We must invest in transformative policies that address systemic racism and create an equitable society."

Exacerbating the growing wealth gap problem, the U.S. Supreme Court blocked President Joe Biden's ambitious student loan forgiveness program to provide up to $20,000 in relief to millions of borrowers. The decision was a blow to the Biden administration's efforts to alleviate the burden of student debt on struggling individuals.

The NAACP Legal Defense Fund reported that borrowers collectively owe more than $1.75 trillion in total student loan debt, with the average borrower owing $28,950 individually. America's racial wealth gap means that the student debt burden falls disproportionately on students of color and their families, with long-term implications.

The significant disparity in wealth between white people and people of color in the United States is known as the racial wealth gap. This gap is striking and staggering. Black households have about seven cents on the dollar compared to white homes, per a 2019 report from the Legal Defense Fund Thurgood Marshall Institute.

The LDF said the stark gap stems from years of entrenched, structural racism. "Racial wealth inequalities in the United States today are a direct result of centuries of racialized, exploitative social and legal structures—policies that set the foundation for a skewed distribution of land, labor, political power, and resource ownership by race. These patterns continue today and are evident in Black-white racial disparities in net worth, known as the Black-white racial wealth gap," TMI's report explained. These wealth disparities then contribute to significant health, education, income, and more disparities.

As students of color begin college, the racial wealth gap often worsens. Because they have fewer socioeconomic resources—less parental and generational wealth, less home equity to finance a loan, and fewer savings—students of color are forced to take on more debt to cover tuition and living expenses to make up for the wealth gap between them and their white peers. Data from the U.S. Department of Education indicates that around 86 percent of Black students take out student loan debt, compared with roughly 68 percent of white students. Black students also typically owe more than white students. Black borrowers take out an average of $39,500 in student loans, while white students borrow an average of $29,900, the LDF reported.

Additionally, the LDF reiterated that the racial gap in student loan debt doesn't just have short-term impacts on students of color. It also contributes to long-term disparities that further intensify the racial wealth gap and diminish educational and socioeconomic equity throughout students' lives—and even for future generations. In fact, a Brookings Institution study found that the Black-white disparity in student loan debt more than tripled just four years after graduation, further eroding Black students' ability to build wealth.

Student loan debt also has long-lasting effects on borrowers' mental health and capacity to thrive. A 2022 ELVTR survey on student loan debt revealed that borrowers experience adverse mental health conditions due to their debt: 56 percent reported experiencing anxiety, while 32 percent reported depression, 20 percent reported insomnia, and 17 percent reported panic attacks. Additionally, over 80 percent of borrowers said their student loan debt had delayed a major life event. With a higher loan burden, Black borrowers, and those from other communities of color undoubtedly disproportionately experience tangible and intangible detrimental consequences of student debt.

Phillip Washington, Jr., a registered investment adviser and Wealth Building Made Simple Podcast host, wrote in an article for the *Dallas Weekly*, an NNPA member newspaper, that the implications of embracing the new economy and closing the wealth gap are far-reaching. "By actively participating in the edges of innovation, Black individuals can become cooperative components of the global movement forward. This movement brings not only wealth but also happiness, peace, and joy. It is an opportunity to shape the future and contribute to a more inclusive and prosperous society."

Closing the wealth gap, Washington noted, also has broader societal implications. When individuals from all backgrounds have equal access to wealth-creation opportunities, it fosters a more equitable society. It dismantles the barriers historically hindering marginalized communities from achieving economic success. By embracing the new economy, Black America can rewrite the narrative and redefine what is possible.

The journey towards closing the wealth gap in Black America requires a continued collective shift in mindset. While external resistance has historically impeded progress, the internet has provided access to information and opportunities like never before. "The resistance we face today is primarily internal, rooted in fear of the unknown," he added.

Are there still biased people in positions of power? Of course, Washington wrote. "There always will be in any majority class's perspective regardless of race, sex, or other classification. The point is the world is moving fast towards a more diverse perspective, and the perceived power of those with a Eurocentric perspective is no longer as strong as most believe it to be. Those of us playing at the edges see nothing but space and opportunity. There are no biases out here, but our own brought in from past memories and stories passed down."

The never-ending wealth gap pushes the reparations narrative. The question of reparations for descendants of enslaved individuals has emerged as a crucial and long-overdue matter. While other communities, such as Holocaust survivors, have received apologies and reparations from the government, the issue of reparations for Black Americans has remained unresolved.

Following the Civil War, General William T. Sherman's Special Field Order No. 15 promised 40 acres of land and a mule to newly freed slaves to give them a foothold for economic independence. However, this promise was short-lived, as the policy was quickly reversed, leaving the descendants of enslaved individuals without the support they were entitled to.

Remarkably, enslavers received reparations through the compensation provided for their lost "property" after the abolition of slavery. Meanwhile, Black Americans endured generations of systemic oppression and discrimination and were left to navigate a world stacked against them.

The United States government has taken steps to acknowledge historical wrongs and provide reparations for various communities impacted by past injustices. Holocaust victims and survivors received apologies and reparations for the unspeakable horrors they endured during World War II. Native American communities have also received compensation for land seizures and other injustices.

The effects of slavery persist in modern America, as evidenced by the enduring wealth gap, disparities in education and healthcare, and a criminal justice system that disproportionately affects Black Americans. Advocates for reparations argue that this legacy of inequality necessitates a concerted effort to rectify historical wrongs.

Efforts to secure reparations for descendants of enslaved individuals are gaining momentum across the country. Various proposals, including the decades-long discussions about H.R. 40, a bill to establish a commission to study and develop reparation, continue on the federal level. Additionally, some local governments have taken steps to implement reparative measures, including financial compensation and initiatives to address economic disparities.

As the nation grapples with its complex history, the question of reparations emerges as a crucial element in achieving true justice and reconciliation. Advocates argue that recognizing the historical and ongoing impacts of slavery is not only a moral imperative but also a necessary step toward a more equitable and inclusive society.

In a nation that values justice and equality, the call for reparations for descendants of enslaved individuals grows stronger by the day. As conversations surrounding this issue continue to gain traction, the question of how America will address its historical injustices remains at the forefront of national discourse.

Officials in Amherst, Massachusetts, announced in October 2023 that they were contemplating accelerating their groundbreaking reparations initiative. Located in the so-called Pioneer Valley of Western Massachusetts, Amherst established one of the nation's first reparation funds for Black residents two years ago, and town officials are now deliberating options to expedite the allocation of the $2 million endowment.

The Amherst Town Council sought to address historical injustices resulting from slavery and discrimination in 2020 in response to widespread protests following the tragic death of George Floyd by Minneapolis police officers. Officials said the fund's inception marked a significant stride towards reconciliation and equity.

The proposed funding plan, equivalent to the annual tax revenue generated from cannabis sales, currently stands at an estimated $200,000 annually. The original strategy entailed a decade-long effort to grow the fund before disbursing up to $100,000 a year in the town where the Black population constitutes approximately 6 percent.

As reported by the Black Press, the Assembly, which the town manager appointed, now favors a potentially shorter timeline. One proposition suggests allocating $100,000 from cannabis tax revenue annually towards reparations. Another option is to achieve the $2 million target in four years rather than the initially envisioned 10.

"The recommendations we've made will begin to make this space one that is more inviting, welcoming, and hospitable for people of African descent," asserted Amilcar Shabazz, a distinguished member of the Assembly and a professor in the W.E.B. Du Bois Department of Afro-American Studies at the University of Massachusetts. Shabazz, who authored a comprehensive book on reparations, emphasized the transformative potential of the endeavor.

Amherst joins a growing roster of American communities, organizations, and institutions committed to providing reparations for Black individuals. The movement spans states like California, cities like Providence, religious denominations including the Episcopal Church, and prestigious colleges such as Georgetown University.

Advocates in Amherst have pointed to Evanston, Illinois, which recently became the first U.S. city to implement reparations. Evanston's program utilizes tax revenues from marijuana sales to provide eligible Black residents with $25,000 housing grants for down payments, repairs, or existing mortgages.

California has made significant strides in the pursuit of reparations, with a task force presenting lawmakers with a report containing over 100 recommendations earlier this year. The exhaustive 1,100-page report meticulously outlines California's historical role in perpetuating discrimination against Black residents. Proposed remedies range from formal apologies to financial restitution for descendants of enslaved individuals impacted by discriminatory policing and housing policies.

In December 2020, the Amherst Town Council adopted the African Heritage Reparation Assembly, which officials called a pivotal step in affirming the town's commitment to ending structural racism and achieving racial equity for Black residents. The Assembly's mandate was to formulate reparations proposals and a comprehensive Municipal Reparations Plan, encompassing both a reparations fund and a community-wide process of reconciliation and repair.

The plan includes eligibility criteria determined and approved by the broader Amherst Black community through a comprehensive census and community feedback process. Additional strategies to combat anti-Black structural and communal racism, such as truth-telling and reconciliation events, will be integrated.

"Collaboration with other groups striving for racial equity in Amherst and engagement with key community stakeholders will be prioritized," officials stated. The case for reparations could easily be seen in the October 2023 death of Hughes Van Ellis, one of the last three survivors of the 1921 Tulsa Race Massacre, who died at 102, according to Oklahoma Democratic Rep. Regina Goodwin, who spoke on behalf of his family.

Known affectionately as "Uncle Redd," Ellis was a World War II war veteran and a symbol of resilience in the face of racial adversity.

Goodwin remarked, "He bravely served America, even as he spent a lifetime awaiting atonement related to the Tulsa Race Massacre, which occurred between May 31 and June 1, 1921, when white mobs violently attacked Black residents, destroying over 35 square blocks of the prosperous Greenwood District, known as 'Black Wall Street.'"

Goodwin, a staunch advocate for reparations for race massacre survivors, emphasized Ellis' unwavering commitment to the cause.

"Two days ago, Mr. Ellis urged us to keep fighting for justice," Goodwin noted. "In the midst of his death, there remains an undying sense of right and wrong. Mr. Ellis was assured we would remain steadfast, and we repeated to him his own words, 'We Are One,' and we lastly expressed our love."

Van Ellis leaves behind his sister Viola Fletcher and Lessie Randle as the last known living survivors of the Tulsa Race Massacre. The Diaspora African Forum (DAF), which adored Ellis and referred to him as Uncle Redd, mourned his passing deeply.

In tribute to his remarkable life and the enduring connection between the African diaspora and their heritage, Van Ellis was granted honorary Ghanaian citizenship. H.E. Dr. Erieka Bennett, Founder and Head of Mission for DAF, and Dr. Toni Luck organized the historic visit of Uncle Redd and Mother Fletcher to Ghana in August 2021.

"Mr. Van Ellis's existence illuminated the indomitable nature of the human spirit amidst overwhelming odds," Dr. Bennett asserted. "Granting him honorary Ghanaian citizenship was a gesture of profound respect for his enduring legacy."

Rocky Dawuni, a three-time Grammy-nominated singer-songwriter and record producer, also saluted Van Ellis.

"Uncle Redd had a larger-than-life presence. Having survived the Tulsa Race Massacre and lived on to a glorious age of 102, his life and story have become part of our collective struggle as a people," Dawuni stated. "His experiences give us a unique glimpse into what black people had to endure and still have to endure to this day."

Uncle Redd's death came just months after the Oklahoma Supreme Court agreed to hear an appeal challenging the dismissal of a lawsuit to secure reparations for the last three remaining survivors of the 1921 Tulsa Race Massacre.

A lower state court dismissed the case in July 2023, prompting the plaintiffs to take the matter to the state's highest judicial authority. Their lawsuit seeks relief for the damages inflicted during the massacre, labeling it a "public nuisance."

The survivors also seek to recover unjust enrichment gained through the exploitation of the tragic event. Judge Caroline Wall dismissed the case with prejudice based on the city's argument that it should not be held liable. The city contended that a mere historical association does not grant the right to seek compensation from any project connected to the Tulsa Race Massacre.

The victims asked the Oklahoma Supreme Court to let them testify before they die. They want to share their experiences of the massacre and how it affected them and the Greenwood community.

The survivors' legal team argued that Judge Wall's ruling imposed an unjust and impractical requirement on parties alleging public nuisance claims.

"If this truly is a nation of laws and a state based on the law, then my clients, the last-known survivors of the massacre, should get the opportunity that no one else who suffered the devastation had the privilege of,"

Damario Solomon-Simmons, National Civil Rights Attorney and founder of Justice for Greenwood, asserted.

He stressed the importance of survivors being able to bring their case to court in order to evaluate the harm and address the problems caused by the widespread destruction.

The lawyers argue that the District Court's ruling requires too much detail in requesting solutions for public nuisance claims, even before the legal proceedings are complete.

This requirement, they argued, is unsupported by Oklahoma's notice pleading code or legal precedent. The lawyers also said that the District Court allowed the city to break a promise made in open court.

In that promise, city officials agreed not to file new motions to dismiss the survivors' claims about unjust enrichment. However, the city filed another motion to dismiss, which the District Court erroneously granted.

"This is a fight for righteous justice and redress. It's not about anything other than advancing this case according to the law as it is written," Solomon-Simmons emphasized.

He called upon the Supreme Court to meticulously review the law and swiftly overturn Wall's erroneous decision to dismiss the case.

Activist and journalist A. Peter Bailey wrote in the Black Press, "It's time for serious Black folks in this country to make it clear that when we advocate for reparations, it is not requesting some kind of gift from the federal government." Reparations to us, Bailey wrote, means that as descendants of enslaved Africans, we are due payment for the 250 years for which our ancestors were forced to work for absolutely no payment. The only thing provided by the enslavers was enough food and clothing to enable our African ancestors to continue working so that the enslavers could fill their pockets with money.

That's why reparations which is defined as "broadly understood compensation given for an abuse or injury." Our enslaved ancestors were not paid for either abuse or injury."

Columnist Courtland Milloy, in a Washington Post column titled, "Fight for reparations widens understanding of history," provided solid comments on reparations from Roslyn Mickens and Kelly Matthews, leaders of the organization DMV Freedmen. According to Ms. Mickens, "We have reached the conclusion that the U.S. Supreme Court will never honor a reparations claim that is rooted in racial terms. ... Reparations is not a cure for racism. This is not about reparations for 'Black' people. Anybody can say that they are 'Black' these days. This is about reparations for the descendants of America's emancipated people. The past is not the past. . . . Racism endures, the legacy of slavery lives on. But a new generation of freedmen will always be there demanding that the nation makes amends."

Ms. Matthews noted, "When America was being built, we were being excluded from economic development. What we got were massacres; were burned, lynched, bombed, drowned, water-logged. Anytime we tried to make it, our Black excellence was met with White violence, Black Codes, convict leasing, school desegregation."

The analysis put forth by Ms. Mickens and Ms. Matthews, based on how America has treated people of African descent, its right on target, Bailey asserted. However, when it comes to reparations, "I have a slight difference with them. I strongly believe that reparations should focus solely on what is owed to the descendants of our African ancestors for 250 years of free, forced labor," he wrote. "Payment for post-slavery labor is a separate issue to be dealt with. Reparations for the direct descendants of those Africans who were forced to work for 250 years without being paid a single penny is absolutely clear. That's why demanding reparations to direct descendants is not requesting a gift from the federal government."

To be sure, there has been progress. In Pittsburgh's Hill District, the historic Bethel African Methodist Episcopal Church will return to its former location. More than 60 years ago, the church was forced to relinquish its sanctuary to an urban renewal project that destroyed the core of an African American neighborhood. The church was compensated for a fraction of its value, according to the church.

Now, the church has reached an agreement with the Pittsburgh Penguins, the NHL team that owns the development rights to the site adjacent to its current facility. According to a report by TheGrio, the Penguins have consented to allowing the church to use a 1.5-acre plot of land that the church plans to use for housing and other revenue-generating development.

Kevin Acklin, president of business operations for the Penguins, stated that the organization is "recognizing our role here as a steward" of the property and its history. Prior to 1967, the Penguins played in a former community arena, and now they play in a newer arena nearby.

According to historians, the Hill District was a center of Black culture in the 20th century, renowned for its jazz clubs and other cultural landmarks depicted in many of acclaimed playwright August Wilson's works. In addition, Bethel AME played an important role in that community. It was founded in 1808 and is regarded as Pittsburgh's oldest Black church. From its inception, it was involved in infant education and civil rights.

It opened a large brick church with rounded arches and a prominent tower in 1906 in the Lower Hill District, which was home to 3,000 members at its zenith.

In the 1950s, the Pittsburgh Urban Redevelopment Authority declared a large portion of Lower Hill to be derelict. It oversaw the demolition of approximately 1,300 structures on 95 acres, displacing more than 8,000 individuals, more than 400 businesses, and numerous places of worship.

Bethel congregants stated that the predominantly white Catholic church was not, however, demolished. Church leaders battled the building's demolition unsuccessfully, ultimately receiving $240,000 for a $745,000 property.

The pastor of Bethel, Rev. Dale Snyder, told TheGrio, "This is a model for how we can heal the broken realities of America." The church intends to construct housing, a daycare center, and other potential commercial developments on the property. The Rev. Prudence Harris, associate pastor and lifelong Bethel member, stated that she was five years old when she and her parents witnessed the deconstruction of the previous sanctuary. The agreement was reached after years of public requests and protests by the church.

It is a microcosm of a larger conflict over the legacy of the 1950s project, in which Black community leaders have long sought redress from Pittsburgh's political, business, and athletic elites. The Penguins hope that the agreement and the extensive efforts to redevelop the site can serve as a model for other U.S. cities with similar urban renewal scars from the mid-20th century.

"I have never been a devotee of hockey," said AME Third District Bishop Erroneous McLoud Jr., who thanked the Penguins for turning him into a hockey fan during a news conference on the site Bethel is acquiring. He stated that this agreement "could and should serve as a model for reparations worldwide."

The accord is a component of broader efforts to collaborate with Hill District residents to restore the neighborhood's former connections to downtown. All of the main parties, including the city, county, and two public authorities, agreed to include Hill District stakeholders in a plan in 2014.

Church leaders stated, "While the agreement is a step toward reparations for the historic Black church and the Hill District, there is still a long way to go in addressing the damage caused in the middle of the 20th century."

In January 2023, officials announced plans for each Black inhabitant of San Francisco, including those arrested during the racist war on drugs, should receive a one-time, lump-sum payment of $5 million from the African American Reparations Advisory Committee. Assuming the city council approves the proposal, it would be the largest payment of reparations in American history.

In a draft proposal for reparations released, members of the San Francisco African American Reparations Advisory Committee noted, "We have ultimately established that the repercussions of numerous programmatic and policy actions by San Francisco's administration have been generational and overlapping."

Committee members asserted that the most prominent period that illustrates how the city and county of San Francisco as an institution contributed to the depletion of Black wealth and the forced relocation of its Black inhabitants was the period of urban renewal.

Further, the committee concluded that "public and private entities facilitated and coddled the conditions that created near-exclusive Black communities within the city, limited political participation and representation, disinvested from academic and cultural institutions, and intentionally displaced Black communities from San Francisco through targeted, sometimes violent actions."

San Francisco's African American population grew rapidly between 1940 and 1963.

To address what the *San Francisco Chronicle* calls "a national racial reckoning," the Board of Supervisors established the AARAC committee in December 2020.

The committee's investigation determined that segregation, structural oppression, and racial prejudice developed from the institution of slavery had a tremendous impact on the development of the city, even though California was never formally a slave state.

Throughout the 20th century, the *Chronicle* reported, "San Francisco was a Ku Klux Klan stronghold, prohibited Black people from residing in particular districts, kept them out of city employment, and bulldozed the Fillmore," a historically Black neighborhood and commercial center. AARAC Chair Eric McDonnell told the newspaper, "Centuries of devastation and destruction of Black lives, Black bodies, and Black communities should be met with centuries of restoration."

This committee's actions are consistent with those of other jurisdictions, where similar bodies have advocated for reparations for African Americans.

Residents must have self-identified as Black or African American on public documents for a minimum of 10 years and be at least 18 years old when the committee's plan is approved to receive the compensation. Additionally, individuals may be required to show that they were born in San Francisco between 1940 and 1996, have been residents of the city for at least 13 years, and are either a former inmate themselves or a direct descendant of a former inmate who served time during the war on drugs.

The *Chronicle* said that "to put that in context," the state reparations task panel believes Black Californians may be awarded $569 billion for housing discrimination alone between 1933 and 1977. Evanston, Illinois, voted to pay $400,000 to select African Americans as part of the city's vow to spend $10 million over a decade on reparations payments shortly after the San Francisco committee was founded.

The government of St. Paul, Minnesota, has apologized for its role in institutional and structural racism and formed a committee to investigate reparations.

A report detailing the committee's proposed financial compensation for African Americans was subsequently made public. A reparations task committee was established by the state of California in 2023, and its report from that year detailed the incalculable harm that slavery had caused to African Americans.

The San Francisco committee recommended that low-income African Americans get an annual payment equivalent to the region median for at least 250 years, on top of the $5 million payout. As an added measure, the city would establish a public bank framework and provide citizens with extensive financial education to ensure that those without bank accounts have access to equal opportunities, including increased access to credit, loans, financing, and other means of managing their money.

The committee also seeks to pay for a broad debt cancellation plan that wipes out all types of debt including student loans, personal loans, credit card debt, and payday loans.

"Given the history of financial institutions preying on underbanked communities—and especially given the vulnerability of subsets of this population such as seniors and youth — this body recommends putting legal parameters and structures in place to ensure access to funds and to mitigate speculative harm done by others," the committee concluded.

Also in 2023, California's reparations task panel approved recommendations to compensate and apologize to Black communities for centuries of discrimination. At a meeting in Oakland, the nine-member committee, which first met nearly two years ago, approved a lengthy list of reparations recommendations for state lawmakers to examine.

At the meeting, U.S. Rep. Barbara Lee (D-Calif.), called on states and the federal government to implement reparations legislation.

Lee said reparations are morally justified and could solve historical racial imbalances and inequality. The panel's first vote accepted a detailed assessment of Black Californian discrimination in voting, housing, education, disproportionate policing and incarceration, and others. Other suggestions included creating a new organization to serve descendants of enslaved people and calculating what the state owes them.

"An apology and an admission of wrongdoing alone is not going to be satisfactory," said Chris Lodgson, an organizer with the Coalition for a Just and Equitable California, a reparations advocacy group. The task force's draft recommendation requires parliamentarians to "censure the gravest barbarities" on behalf of the state in their apologies.

The task force noted that California's first elected governor, Peter Hardeman Burnett, was a white supremacist who supported legislation excluding Black people from the state.

The draft report states that California, a "free" state since 1850, did not pass any laws guaranteeing freedom for all. Instead, the state Supreme Court enforced the federal Fugitive Slave Act for over a decade until freedom arrived in U.S. states.

"By participating in these horrors, California further perpetuated the harms African Americans faced, imbuing racial prejudice throughout society through segregation, public and private discrimination, and unequal state and federal funding," the study authors wrote.

The task team adopted a public apology, admitting the state's past wrongs and committing not to repeat them. It would be presented to the descendants of enslaved people.

California apologized for interning Japanese Americans and mistreating Native Americans.

The panel adopted the draft report's "cash or its equivalent" restitution for qualified residents.

Oakland's Mills College of Northeastern University hosted over 100 citizens and activists. All lamented the country's "broken promise" to give emancipated slaves 40 acres and a mule.

Many claimed it was time for governments to fix the harms that prevented African Americans from living without fear of being wrongly punished, maintaining property, and earning wealth. Former Black Panther Party chairwoman Elaine Brown encouraged protests.

The task force meeting was viewed as a pivotal moment in the push for local, state, and federal agencies to apologize for African American discrimination.

"There's no way in the world that many of these recommendations are going to get through because of the inflationary impact," said University of San Diego School of Law professor and reparations specialist Roy L. Brooks. Economists predict the state may owe Black residents $800 billion, or 2.5 times its yearly budget. The newest task force draft report has a much lower figure.

In 2020, Secretary of State Shirley Weber, a former Democratic assemblymember, authored legislation creating the task force to address the state's historical culpability for African American harms, not as a substitute for federal reparations.

The task team initially limited reparations to descendants of 19th-century enslaved or free Black individuals. As reparations for African Americans have had uneven success elsewhere, the group's work has received national attention.

Black residents in the Chicago suburb of Evanston, Illinois, recently received housing vouchers as reparations, but few reportedly used them.

A bill to acknowledge the inhumanity of slavery in New York and form a panel to investigate reparations proposals has cleared the Assembly but not the Senate.

A decades-old federal proposal to form a reparations panel for African Americans has stalled in Congress. Oakland City Council member Kevin Jenkins called the California task group "a powerful example" of what can happen when people work together.

Jenkins stated, "I am confident that through our collective efforts, we can significantly advance reparations in our great state of California and, ultimately, the country."

After George Floyd was murdered, the District of Columbia City Council announced it would create a task team to investigate compensation. Legislators in both Maryland and Virginia have expressed an interest in researching reparations. Meanwhile, there has been no movement on a federal level on a bill by Texas Democrat Rep. Sheila Jackson Lee to establish a committee to investigate reparations.

Additionally, in the summer of 2023, the Black Press was able to proclaim that reparations have finally arrived for some Black Americans. The city of Evanston, Illinois, began its historic reparations program by providing compensation to its many of its Black residents. Checks and vouchers in the amount of $25,000 have been sent to eligible residents, a move that backs up the city's 2019 promise to pay as much as $10 million over the next decade in reparations. Approved in March 2021, the program targets Black residents who resided in Evanston between 1919 and 1969 or experienced housing discrimination due to the city's policies. It's a similar program which officials in San Francisco currently are grappling with, as that California city also considers reparations by the harms suffered by Black residents denied fair housing, job and educational opportunities, and other hardships that were unfairly inflicted upon African American communities.

One Evanston recipient, Louis Weathers, an 88-year-old retired postal worker and Korean War veteran, shared his personal experience with racial prejudice during his interview with the *Wall Street Journal*. He recounted his time at an integrated junior high school, where a white teacher consistently marginalized Black students.

He explained that the teacher would purposely ignore their raised hands to undermine their capabilities. "We got onto that, though. When we didn't know the answer, we raised our hands," recounted Weathers, who was among the first to receive a $25,000 check from the city. He told the newspaper that he gave his reparations check to his son to reduce debt and make upgrades on his home. The payments, which can be received as vouchers or cash, are funded through taxes on marijuana and real-estate transfers.

While Evanston has begun making reparation payments, similar proposals at the national level have faced challenges.

Although a federal bill calling for a national reparations task force has been introduced annually since 1989, it has yet to be voted on in Congress. Evanston's mayor, Daniel Biss, said his city remains committed to change. "Our job here is just to move forward and to continue being that example, to continue illustrating that a small municipality can make real tangible progress," he stated.

CHAPTER FIFTEEN

Redlining, Gentrification, and the Stealing of Communities

"Not everything that is faced can be changed, but nothing can be changed until it is faced."

—JAMES BALDWIN

"People bury the parts of history they don't like, pave it over like African cemeteries beneath Manhattan skyscrapers."

—ALYSSA COLE, *When No One Is Watching*

R edlining stands as a testament to the enduring legacy of systemic racism. This discriminatory practice, born in the early 20th century, systematically curtailed financial resources, housing opportunities, and economic mobility for African American communities. Understanding its historical roots, methods, and lingering effects is crucial to comprehending the profound toll it has taken.

The early 20th century bore witness to the Great Migration, a mass exodus of millions of African Americans from the Southern states to Northern cities, driven by the promise of economic opportunities and an escape from racial violence. This demographic shift led to overcrowded urban areas, exacerbating racial tensions and the government and private industry enforcing racial bias and segregation.

In the 1930s, the federal government introduced a system to assess lending risk in urban areas through the Home Owners' Loan Corporation (HOLC). The HOLC produced color-coded maps categorizing sites based on perceived lending risks to evaluate neighborhoods. This categorization, however, was steeped in racial bias, codifying discriminatory practices that would endure for decades.

The HOLC's color-coded maps, known as "redlining maps," divided neighborhoods into four categories: green (low risk), blue (moderate risk), yellow (high risk), and red (highest risk). The criteria for these designations were deeply flawed, relying heavily on racial composition. Areas with African American populations were invariably marked red, effectively branding them as financial no-go zones.

The Federal Housing Administration (FHA) introduced redlining in the 1930s as a government-approved practice of discriminating against minority communities by denying them access to housing loans and mortgages. This deliberate policy created segregated neighborhoods and stifled economic mobility for generations. The scars of redlining are still visible in neighborhoods across America in places where the lack of investment and resources has limited opportunities for residents.

Simultaneously, private industry and local governments enforced restrictive covenants and contractual agreements barring homeowners from selling or renting to African Americans. Though legally unenforceable after the 1948 Shelley v. Kraemer Supreme Court decision, these covenants persisted in practice for years.

Redlining deprived African Americans of the opportunity to accumulate wealth through homeownership. As redlined neighborhoods were systematically denied loans and investments, property values stagnated or plummeted, perpetuating cycles of poverty.

The impact of redlining extended beyond housing, affecting access to quality education and employment opportunities. Disinvested communities faced underfunded schools and limited job prospects, perpetuating systemic inequalities.

Redlined neighborhoods often bear the brunt of environmental hazards and lack adequate healthcare resources. This ecological injustice further exacerbates health disparities within African American communities.

Though officially dismantled, redlining continues to cast a long shadow over African American communities. Its enduring effects are felt in wealth disparities, educational inequalities, and healthcare injustices. Acknowledging this dark chapter in American history is essential to pursuing a more just and equitable society. It is a call to action, urging us to confront the past and work towards a future free from the shackles of systemic racism.

As Black Press writer Barrington Salmon noted in a 2023 article, in addition to keeping communities white, redlining robbed African Americans of countless millions—perhaps billions—of dollars since the practice was codified because of lending and real estate discrimination and disinvestment.

It would be safe to assume that in 2023, redlining is a thing of the past consigned to the proverbial dustbin of history, but to think so would be wrong.

"Now it's not as obvious or explicit, but redlining is extremely pervasive and prevalent in society today," an official from the U.S. Department of Housing and Urban Development (HUD) told Salmon. "The prevalence hasn't changed. We fight every day to effect change. We have to be diligent in our efforts to fight it."

Redlining's corrosive legacy persists in discriminatory lending, inequities, and disparities in housing practices and how homes are financed, Salmon continued. Ultimately, all this has a broad impact on homeownership, the value of homes, and especially the net worth of African American families and individuals.

At the end of the Second World War, the United States faced a significant housing demand as American servicemen and women returned home and wanted to buy homes and raise their families. In response, the Federal Housing Administration (FHA) expanded its ability to provide financing and insurance loans. The feds backing lenders and developers reduced risk to banks and those offering mortgages and construction loans.

"The lower risk to lenders resulted in lower interest rates, which granted middle-class people the ability to borrow money to purchase homes," said Rajeh Saadeh, a real estate and civil rights attorney, in a Banknote story about redlining. "With the new lending policies and larger potential homeowner pool, real estate developers bought huge tracts of land just outside urban areas and developed them by building numerous homes and turning the areas into today's suburbs."

However, many of these new developments had restrictive covenants that barred Black people from buying these homes. Meanwhile, in those parts of cities where large numbers of non-whites lived, the redlining, Saadeh explained, made "them ineligible for federally backed mortgages (which effectively meant, for affordable mortgages, period)."

"Consequently, people of color could not get loans to buy property in the suburbs; nor could they borrow to purchase homes in areas in where they were concentrated," the attorney, a former real estate law professor, said.

Saadeh said the ramification of America's "systemic, codified policy by the government, mortgage lenders, real estate developers, and real estate agents as a bloc to deprive Black people of homeownership . . . has been generational."

Andre M. Perry, a senior fellow at the Brookings Institution, and his colleague David Harshbarger, a former research analyst with the Metropolitan Policy Program, co-wrote in a 2019 report titled: "America's Formerly Redlined Neighborhoods Have Changed, and So Must Solutions to Rectify Them." The report explained that the past continues to haunt the present.

Any declarations that redlining has ended have repeatedly been proven premature "Together with racially restrictive housing covenants that prohibited Black Americans from buying certain properties, redlining prevented generations of families from gaining equity in homeownership or making improvements to homes already owned," the report read. "These unjust practices form part of a long history of discrimination, which has contributed to the disparities in homeownership and wealth still observed between the Black and White populations of the country today."

Even with the passage of the Fair Housing Act in 1968, a range of other forms of discriminatory housing practices have reared their ugly heads. For example, housing experts have documented what some characterize as "reverse redlining," where banks have engaged in predatory lending in Black and Latino neighborhoods that once were legally redlined. One of the primary reasons for the housing crash in 2008 was mortgage lenders enticing low-income borrowers with hundreds of thousands of risky subprime loans, including "no-doc" and balloon-payment loans. Consequently, about half of Black homeowners and a third of Latino homeowners lost their homes, and both communities have yet to recover fully.

The HUD representative said agency officials and staff use analytical metrics to uncover evidence of redlining. Where HUD finds, lenders aren't lending to marginalized communities, they force the implementation of remedies and investments in affected communities. The official said HUD has also taken a more exhaustive, comprehensive look at different elements of the housing ecosystem, such as appraisals. Recently, there have been several stories about appraisers who value the homes and land of African Americans for hundreds of thousands of dollars less because the owners are Black.

"Redlining is just one of many aspects of Fair Lending aspects. "Appraisals," the HUD official said, "inform the lender of what the property is worth. There has been a historic undervaluing of communities of color, and that continues to be pervasive. We're looking at agents and brokers. It's a big task."

"HUD is definitely taking a hard look at the appraiser ecosystem looking for unnecessary barriers to entry, ways to increase diversity, and how to make it easier for Blacks to get into an almost all-white industry."

In early 2023, The Justice Department announced the launch of the department's new Combatting Redlining Initiative today. Redlining is an illegal practice in which lenders avoid providing services to individuals living in communities of color because of the race or national origin of the people who live in those communities. The new Initiative represents the department's most aggressive and coordinated enforcement effort to address redlining, which is prohibited by the Fair Housing Act and the Equal Credit Opportunity Act.

"Lending discrimination runs counter to fundamental promises of our economic system," said Attorney General Merrick B. Garland. "When people are denied credit simply because of their race or national origin, their ability to share in our nation's prosperity is all but eliminated. Today, we are committing ourselves to addressing modern-day redlining by making far more robust use of our fair lending authorities. We will spare no resource to ensure that federal fair lending laws are vigorously enforced and that financial institutions provide equal opportunity for every American to obtain credit."

"Enforcement of our fair lending laws is critical to ensure that banks and lenders are providing communities of color equal access to lending opportunities," said Assistant Attorney General Kristen Clarke for the Justice Department's Civil Rights Division. "Equal and fair access to mortgage lending opportunities is the cornerstone on which families and communities can build wealth in our country. We know well that redlining is not a problem from a bygone era but a practice that remains pervasive in the lending industry today. Our new Initiative should send a strong message to banks and lenders that we will hold them accountable as we work to combat discriminatory race and national origin-based lending practices."

Redlining, a practice institutionalized by the federal government during the New Deal era and implemented then and now by private lenders, has had a lasting negative impact. For American families, homeownership remains the principal means of building wealth, and the deprivation of investment in and access to mortgage lending services for communities of color have contributed to families of color persistently lagging behind in homeownership rates and net worth compared to white families. The gap in homeownership rates between White and Black families is larger today than it was in 1960, before the passage of the Fair Housing Act of 1968.

This initiative, which will be led by the Civil Rights Division's Housing and Civil Enforcement Section in partnership with U.S. Attorney's Offices, will build on the longstanding work by the division that seeks to make mortgage credit and homeownership accessible to all Americans on the same terms, regardless of race or national origin and regardless of the neighborhood where they live. The DOJ said the initiative would:

⊙ Utilize U.S. Attorneys' Offices as force multipliers to ensure that fair lending enforcement is informed by local expertise on housing markets and the credit needs of local communities of color.

⊙ Expand the department's analyses of potential redlining to both depository and non-depository institutions. Non-depository lenders are not traditional banks and do not provide typical banking services but engage in mortgage lending and now make the majority of mortgages in this country.

⊙ Strengthen our partnership with financial regulatory agencies to ensure the identification and referrals of fair lending violations to the Department of Justice.

⊙ Increase coordination with State Attorneys General on potential fair lending violations.

In addition to the Initiative announcement, the Justice Department, the U.S. Attorney's Office for the Western District of Tennessee, the Consumer Financial Protection Bureau (CFPB) and the Office of the Comptroller of the Currency (OCC) announced an agreement to resolve allegations that Trustmark National Bank engaged in lending discrimination by redlining predominantly Black and Hispanic neighborhoods in Memphis, Tennessee.

The parties' proposed consent order was filed today in conjunction with a complaint in the U.S. District Court for the Western District of Tennessee. The complaint alleges that Trustmark National Bank violated the Fair Housing Act and the Equal Credit Opportunity Act, which prohibit financial institutions from discriminating on the basis of race, color or national origin in their mortgage lending services. The complaint also alleges that Trustmark National Bank violated the Consumer Financial Protection Act, which prohibits offering or providing to a consumer any financial product or service not in conformity with federal consumer financial law.

Specifically, the complaint alleges that, from 2014 to 2018, Trustmark engaged in unlawful redlining in Memphis by avoiding predominantly Black and Hispanic neighborhoods because of the race, color, and national origin of the people living in, or seeking credit for properties in, those neighborhoods. The complaint also alleges that Trustmark's branches were concentrated in majority-White neighborhoods, that the bank's loan officers did not serve the credit needs of majority-Black and Hispanic neighborhoods, that Trustmark's outreach and marketing avoided those neighborhoods, and that Trustmark's internal fair-lending policies and procedures were inadequate to ensure that the bank provided equal access to credit to communities of color.

The department opened its investigation after one of Trustmark's regulators, the OCC, referred the matter. Trustmark has fully cooperated in this investigation and amicably resolved the allegations.

"Trustmark purposely excluded and discriminated against Black and Hispanic communities," said Director Rohit Chopra of the Consumer Financial Protection Bureau (CFPB). "The federal government will be working to rid the market of racist business practices, including those by discriminatory algorithms."

"Home ownership is the foundation of economic success for most American families," said Acting U.S. Attorney Joseph C. Murphy Jr. for the Western District of Tennessee. "Fair lending practices required by federal law—and the enforcement of those laws—ensure a better future for all Americans. Our office believes that enforcement actions of this type are essential to fair lending system that benefits everyone, and we will continue to prioritize these cases."

"The OCC has had a long history of strong partnership with the Justice Department's Housing and Civil Enforcement Section of the Civil Rights Division, referring potential fair lending violations and sharing our extensive examiner, economist and legal findings, as we did in the Trustmark matter," said Acting Comptroller of the Currency Michael J. Hsu. "Today's announcement is important because it signifies the unified and unmitigated focus that each of our agencies has placed on the enforcement of the Fair Housing Act and the Equal Credit Opportunity Act. Our collective efforts are critical to addressing the discriminatory lending practices that create and reinforce racial inequity in the financial system."

Under the proposed consent order:

⊙ Trustmark will invest $3.85 million in a loan subsidy fund to increase credit opportunities for current and future residents of predominantly Black and Hispanic neighborhoods in the Memphis area; dedicate at least four mortgage loan officers or community lending specialists to these neighborhoods; and open a loan production office in a majority-Black and Hispanic neighborhood in Memphis.

⊙ Trustmark will devote $400,000 to developing community partnerships to provide services to residents of majority-Black and Hispanic neighborhoods in Memphis that increase access to residential mortgage credit.

⊙ Trustmark will devote at least $200,000 per year to advertising, outreach, consumer financial education and credit repair initiatives in and around Memphis.

⊙ Trustmark will pay a total civil money penalty of $5 million to the OCC and CFPB.

⊙ Trustmark already has established a Fair Lending Oversight Committee and designated a Community Lending Manager who will oversee these efforts and work in close consultation with the bank's leadership.

In August 2021, the department announced a redline settlement with Cadence Bank. Under the settlement, Cadence will invest over $5.5 million to increase credit opportunities for residents of majority-Black and Hispanic neighborhoods in Houston.

In addition to redlining, gentrification has also held back the American Dream from African Americans.

Gentrification, a process often defined by the influx of wealthier residents, rising property values, and the transformation of urban landscapes, has left an indelible mark on American cities over the past several decades. While the term gentrification was coined in the 1960s, its roots trace back further, intertwining with a history of racial and economic disparities in the United States.

As a formal concept, Gentrification originated in the 1964 essay "London: Aspects of Change" by sociologist Ruth Glass, who described the displacement of working-class communities by more affluent residents in London. However, this phenomenon mirrors the United States' history of urban renewal programs from the 1950s to the 1970s, disproportionately impacting African American communities. Neighborhoods like Harlem in New York and Bronzeville in Chicago experienced extensive disruption as part of these urban renewal efforts, leading to the displacement of long-standing residents.

The displacement of marginalized communities marks the legacy of gentrification in the United States, often among African Americans. It has contributed to the erosion of cultural identity and community cohesion in historically Black neighborhoods. The redevelopment of these areas frequently results in the loss of affordable housing, leading to the forced migration of many residents.

As a result, gentrification has frequently exacerbated economic disparities. A study by the National Community Reinvestment Coalition found that gentrified neighborhoods often see a decline in the African American population. The report also highlighted a pattern where displaced African American residents have difficulty returning to these areas due to rising housing costs, thus intensifying housing and economic disparities.

Gentrification continues to shape urban landscapes across the United States, with cities like San Francisco, Washington, D.C., and Portland experiencing significant transformations. In these cases, housing prices have skyrocketed, pushing out long-term residents who can no longer afford to live in their own neighborhoods.

African American communities have borne the brunt of these changes. A report from the Urban Institute noted that in Washington, D.C., the percentage of Black residents in certain neighborhoods decreased significantly while the proportion of White residents increased. These trends are often driven by an influx of higher-income, predominantly White residents and the development of upscale amenities, which displace lower-income African American residents.

To address the negative impacts of gentrification on African American communities, many cities have implemented affordable housing policies, rent control measures, and community land trusts. These efforts seek to protect vulnerable residents and preserve the character of neighborhoods undergoing gentrification. In some cases, local governments have also invested in job training programs and educational initiatives to help long-term residents cope with rising living costs.

However, the challenges of gentrification remain complex, and there is ongoing debate regarding the effectiveness of these measures. Critics argue that the underlying causes of gentrification, such as economic inequality and systemic racism, must be addressed more comprehensively to tackle the issue at its roots.

Gentrification's history is intertwined with the broader context of racial and economic disparities in the United States. Its legacy is displacement, disruption, and disproportionately impacting African American communities. As gentrification continues to reshape the urban landscape, efforts to mitigate its negative consequences are essential to ensure that vulnerable residents are not left behind in urban renewal.

As the Black Press reported in 2020, from a dowdy provincial city in the 1980s, Philadelphia has become a world-class urban center through gentrification—primarily through landmark architecture that now sets the city center and University City apart.

"Over 50, and retirees are moving back from the suburbs where they raised their children into Center City and the Italian Market where I have lived since 1980," stated Dr. Margaret J. King, the director of The Center for Cultural Studies & Analysis in Philadelphia.

"Of course, gentrification brings money into the city, while it also drives up home prices—some houses have multiplied their asking prices 15 times over 40 years," King noted.

"Housing is being restored and renovated, making more of the city habitable and in fact desirable. Now the suburbs have flipped into a working-class magnet as well as a market for Millennials who can't afford center-city prices yet," King stated.

Gentrification isn't just an issue in Philadelphia—not by a long shot.

According to a March 2019 study by the National Community Reinvestment Coalition (NCRC), more than 135,000 Black and Hispanics around the nation were displaced between 2000 and 2012.

Gentrification and displacement of long-time residents were most intense from 2000 to 2013 in the nation's biggest cities, and rare in most other places, according to the study.

During those years, gentrification was concentrated in larger cities with vibrant economies. It also appeared in smaller cities, often impacting areas with the most amenities near central business districts.

In Washington, D.C., 20,000 Black residents were displaced, and in Portland, Oregon, 13 percent of the Black community was displaced over the more than-decade period that was studied.

Seven cities accounted for nearly half of the gentrification nationally: New York City, Los Angeles, Washington, D.C., Philadelphia, Baltimore, San Diego, and Chicago.

Washington, D.C., was the most gentrified city by a percentage of eligible neighborhoods that experienced gentrification; New York City was the most gentrified by sheer volume, study authors noted.

According to the Merriam-Webster Dictionary, gentrification is defined as the process of repairing and rebuilding homes and businesses in a deteriorating area, such as an urban neighborhood, accompanied by an influx of middle-class or affluent people, and that often results in the displacement of earlier, usually poorer residents.

"Gentrification is rich people deciding they want a specific neighborhood as their own, and they get municipal backing, pay some money, and get all of the poor people out of there," stated Mark Love, a New York realtor. As predominantly minority neighborhoods were denied investment and resources, they fell into disrepair.

Neighborhoods were considered eligible to gentrify if in 2000 they were in the lower 40 percent of home values and family incomes in that metropolitan area. During the study, researchers found that most low- to moderate-income neighborhoods did not gentrify or revitalize. Instead, they remained impoverished, untouched by investments and building booms that occurred in major cities, and vulnerable to future gentrification and displacement.

"When a neighborhood gentrifies, the cost of living increases, and it's harder for low-income families to find housing, and that's one of the biggest downsides," stated Melanie Musson, a writer for Expert Insurance Reviews.com.

"In a city like Philadelphia, neighborhoods are part of your identity. If you grow up in a neighborhood, you often want to remain living there your whole life because it's who you are," Musson stated.

"Unfortunately, sometimes, after several generations living in the same zip code, the newest generation has to find housing elsewhere because it's too expensive to live where their home has always been," she said.

Bruce Mirken, the media relations director for the nonprofit public, policy, and advocacy organization, The Greenlining Institute, said he lives in San Francisco and works in Oakland—two cities that are ground zero for the gentrification crisis in California.

"We see the most obvious results among the very low-income, who increasingly cannot keep a roof over their heads, leading to a growing homeless population," Mirken stated.

"And homelessness in California has a distinct racial dynamic, tracing back through a long history of redlining and discrimination: Black Californians represent about six and a half percent of our state's population, but about 40 percent of its homeless," he noted.

In New York, where many residents are still growing accustomed to the decades-long gentrification of Harlem, the Bronx has forever been known as the city's most urban borough. That's quickly changing due to gentrification.

In November 2019, officials announced a $950 million, 4.3 acre, multi-tower, and mixed-use development along the Mott Haven waterfront. More than 1,300 high-end apartments were among the upgrades that were certain to price many long-time residents out of the area.

Mychal Johnson, a co-founding member of South Bronx Unite, told *The Bronx Times* that gentrification isn't good for economically oppressed communities of color.

"It seems like the community board and borough president isn't looking out for the community," Johnson stated.

Shekinah Mitchell, the Neighborhood Partnerships Manager for the Virginia Local Initiatives Support Corporation, wrote an article about a 2019 NCRC study on gentrification and cultural displacement, noting that Richmond, the former capital of the Confederacy, has a history "steeped in racial oppression, inequality, and injustice."

Mitchell had also noted that in 2016, Richmond had similar numbers of Black and White residents. From 2000 to 2016, the Black population decreased by seven percent, while the White population increased by 35 percent.

In 2000, Blacks were 57 percent of the population, and Whites were 38 percent. In 2016, Blacks represented 47 percent, and Whites were 46 percent of the population.

"This shift has come to the East End like a racialized wave crashing onto the shores of the neighborhood in currents of physical, cultural, and economic displacement. The Black community is drowning as we watch our land and culture swallowed up, block by block, with no reprieve in sight," Mitchell wrote in the report.

"Gentrification in the East End of Richmond is manifesting as a process of re-segregation," she stated. "In Richmond, gentrification is colonization."

In Portland, Oregon, an essay that accompanied the NCRC study noted that city as the "Whitest city of its size in the United States."

It said the city's White population currently stands at 77.4 percent, while Blacks comprise just 5.7 percent.

"Take a group of people who have been systematically denied wealth-building opportunities for generations, add low, stagnating incomes, throw in a subprime mortgage disaster, spiraling housing costs, and wholesale community displacement, and you have a recipe for a severe economic backslide," Cheryl Chandler-Roberts, executive director of Portland's African American Alliance for Homeownership, said in the report.

"There is no African American community in Portland at this point," Chandler-Roberts had stated. "It's a scattered community."

With redlining and gentrification, the indelible legacy of the transatlantic slave trade continues to shape American society. This terrible, inhumane, four-century chapter forcibly dispossessed millions of Africans and established the groundwork for deeply entrenched racial inequities. Today, echoes of this legacy persist in the insidious practices of redlining and gentrification, which have left an indelible mark on the socioeconomic landscape of America. These practices stand as stark reminders of the systemic injustices woven into the fabric of American history.

The transatlantic slave trade, a harrowing chapter in human history, forcibly transported Africans to the Americas, subjecting them to unimaginable suffering, exploitation, and inhumane conditions. The mass displacement sowed the seeds of a deeply entrenched system of racial hierarchy with African Americans relegated to the bottom rung. The enduring trauma of this era permeates through generations, shaping African Americans lived experiences and opportunities to this day.

The Southern States'economy flourished on the backs of enslaved Africans, driving immense wealth for White landowners. This brutal system perpetuated racial divisions and laid the groundwork for enduring socioeconomic disparities. It was a system that thrived on the dehumanization and exploitation of a people, leaving an indelible scar on the nation's history. The echoes of this economic exploitation continue to reverberate as disparities in wealth and opportunity persist along racial lines.

The abolition of slavery did not usher in an era of equality. Formerly enslaved people faced systemic discrimination, limited resource access, and a dearth of land ownership opportunities. Jim Crow laws, which represented legalized segregation, further solidified a rigid racial caste system. This era of oppression left an enduring mark on African American communities, creating a legacy of disadvantage extending far beyond those directly affected lifetimes. Generations continue to grapple with the far-reaching consequences of this historical injustice.

Confronting the legacies of exploitation is an essential step toward dismantling the profoundly entrenched inequalities that persist in America today. To bridge this divide, we must advocate for policies that address historical injustices, invest in marginalized communities, and ensure that the benefits of economic growth are shared equitably. Acknowledging the resilience and contributions of those affected by these practices is paramount to creating a more inclusive and just society for all. Only through collective efforts can we begin to rectify the lasting impact of redlining and gentrification, moving towards a future where opportunity and prosperity are accessible to every American, regardless of their racial background.

As we reflect on the enduring legacies of the transatlantic slave trade, it is imperative that we not only acknowledge the deep wounds of the past but also commit to healing them. Redlining and gentrification, born from this history, persist as modern-day instruments of inequality. The responsibility lies with us to dismantle these structures and forge a path toward a more equitable future. By confronting the ghosts of our collective past, we can build a society where everyone has an equal opportunity to thrive, irrespective of their racial heritage. This work, *The Transatlantic Slave Trade: Overcoming the 500-Year Legacy* covering the years 1500–2024, is not just an education and commercial endeavor. It is a call to awaken our awareness and a call to action to achieve a more just and inclusive America.

The transatlantic slave trade also left an indelible mark on the economic landscape of the United States. While it provided immense financial gains for America and various institutions, including churches and universities, its legacy continues to cast a long shadow, contributing to economic disparities that persist for African Americans today.

For five centuries, it involved the forced migration of millions of Africans to the Americas, primarily for labor on plantations. This economic system fueled the growth of industries, particularly agriculture, in the United States. Plantations, predominantly in the South, became economic powerhouses, producing cash crops like tobacco, cotton, and sugar, which were crucial exports.

The economic impact of the transatlantic slave trade on America was profound. The forced labor of enslaved Africans formed the backbone of the agricultural economy, driving unprecedented growth and wealth accumulation. Cotton, in particular, became a cornerstone of the Southern economy, driving innovation in manufacturing and trade. Indirectly, this economic prosperity reverberated nationwide, contributing to developing industries and infrastructure.

Financial institutions, too, profited immensely from the slave trade. Banks in the North provided loans to plantation owners, profiting from the plantation system's success. Moreover, insurance companies thrived by underwriting policies for slave ships, further entwining the financial sector with the perpetuation of slavery.

The economic prosperity derived from the transatlantic slave trade did not translate into generational wealth for African Americans. After emancipation, formerly enslaved individuals were left without resources, facing systemic barriers to economic advancement. Discriminatory practices, such as Jim Crow laws and redlining, continued to inhibit access to education, employment, and housing.

Today, the economic effects of this historical injustice are still palpable. The racial wealth gap persists, with African American families holding only a fraction of the wealth of their white counterparts. Limited access to quality education, employment opportunities, and homeownership are among the enduring challenges faced by African American communities stemming from the legacy of slavery.

Recognizing the economic legacy of the transatlantic slave trade is essential for addressing ongoing disparities. Efforts to rectify this historical injustice include targeted policies for wealth redistribution, access to quality education, and initiatives promoting homeownership. Additionally, fostering economic opportunities in marginalized communities is crucial for dismantling systemic barriers.

In understanding the profound economic impact of the transatlantic slave trade, we confront a painful truth: the legacy of slavery continues to shape economic outcomes for African Americans today. By acknowledging this historical injustice, we can work towards a more equitable and inclusive future for all Americans.

CHAPTER SIXTEEN

The News Media Perpetuates Racism

"If you're not careful, the newspapers will have you hating the people who are being oppressed and loving the people who are doing the oppressing."

—MALCOLM X

"We younger Negro artists who create now intend to express our individual dark-skinned selves without fear or shame. If white people are pleased, we are glad. If they are not, it doesn't matter. We know we are beautiful."

—LANGSTON HUGHES, poet and writer, 1926

An in-depth study by the Pew Research Center in October 2023 took a deep dive into the experiences of Black Americans with news coverage, shedding light on critical perspectives and recommendations for more equitable representation. The survey involved 4,742 U.S. adults identifying as Black and offered an extensive and comprehensive insight into their attitudes, habits, and experiences with news and information.

The findings reveal a stark divide in how Black individuals perceive news coverage of their community. As one participant noted, *"There's not a lot of African American coverage unless it's February or it's criminal."* That sentiment was echoed by another respondent who stated, *"They overemphasize the bad, and not some of the good things that are happening in the community, or if they do talk about the good things, it's just a blurb and they want to focus on the one thing [that] was just terrible."*

Almost two-thirds (63 percent) believe that news about Black people is often portrayed in a negative light compared to other racial and ethnic groups. Furthermore, a significant 57 percent feel that the news only focuses on specific segments of the Black community, while just 9 percent believe it covers a diverse range of individuals.

Half of the respondents expressed dissatisfaction with the coverage, asserting that it often needs vital information, whereas only 9 percent believe it provides a comprehensive picture. Disturbingly, 43 percent claim that the coverage tends to stereotype Black individuals, contrasting starkly with the 11 percent who disagree. The critical views transcended age, gender, and political affiliations and painted a consistent picture of discontent.

According to the survey, 39 percent of Black Americans frequently encounter news that is racist or racially insensitive towards their community, while an additional 41 percent report occasional exposure. The respondents identified various factors contributing to this problem, including media outlets pushing agendas (51 percent, journalists' lack of informed perspectives (45 percent), and the presence of racist views within news organizations (42 percent).

Despite the prevailing skepticism, only 14 percent of Black Americans are highly confident that fair representation in news coverage will occur within their lifetimes. A notable 64 percent of those who have witnessed racially insensitive coverage believe that educating all journalists about issues affecting Black Americans would be an extremely or very effective way to ensure fairer coverage. As one participant emphasized, "There's definitely less empathy, I think, for people of color, for working-class people from people who are not Black. . . . I think they deliver the news in a way that is different than how someone who does understand our experiences would deliver the news."

Substantial percentages also advocate for including more Black voices as sources (54 percent) and for hiring Black individuals in leadership roles within newsrooms (53 percent). That echoed the call for diversification in newsrooms made over five decades ago by the 1967 Kerner Commission.

These findings resonate with the observations of the 1967 Kerner Commission, which highlighted sensationalist, divisive, and inaccurate representations of Black communities in the media. The Commission emphasized the urgent need to diversify newsrooms, a call that remains relevant more than five decades later.

While many Black Americans value the perspective of Black journalists in reporting on racial issues, only 14 percent consider it highly important for news in general to come from Black journalists. Just 15 percent believe a journalist's race is an extremely or very important factor in determining a story's credibility, ranking below factors such as cited sources (53 percent), multiple outlets (50 percent), and the news outlet itself (46 percent.

Diverging opinions emerge when considering the importance of racial identity among Black Americans. Those who place a high value on their Black identity expressed a significantly stronger preference for journalists who understand the historical context of stories involving Black individuals (82 percent). Conversely, this dropped to 55 percent among those who attach less importance to their racial identity.

The study also identified generational and educational divides in perceptions of Black journalists' effectiveness. Younger Black adults, aged 18 to 29, were more likely to believe that Black journalists excel at covering issues related to race (54 percent) and understanding them (50 percent) compared to their older counterparts. Likewise, individuals with higher levels of formal education and income expressed more positive views toward the work of Black journalists.

The Pew Research Center study provided a comprehensive examination of the experiences, opinions, and recommendations of Black Americans regarding news coverage. It underscored the urgent need for reform and emphasized the enduring importance of diverse voices in shaping a fair and accurate narrative. The study showed that the journey towards equitable representation in news coverage remains ongoing, yet the voices and experiences of Black Americans offered a vital guide toward progress.

In an era of rapid information dissemination, the media's influence in shaping public opinion and societal perspectives is unparalleled. However, an alarming pattern persists: a growing chorus asserts that today's news media systemically perpetuates bias against African Americans. This bias finds its origins in the historical wounds of the transatlantic slave trade, an abyss of human suffering that remains an indelible stain on the annals of history. Its brutal legacy has seeped into contemporary society, weaving a complex tapestry of systemic disparities that persist. From economic inequalities to educational injustices, the echoes of this heinous chapter continue to reverberate, infiltrating even the most ostensibly objective institutions, including the media.

African Americans have long grappled with a quest for authentic representation within the media landscape. Studies reveal a glaring chasm in portrayal, often casting African Americans in an unfavorable light, thereby reinforcing detrimental stereotypes. The absence of African American perspectives within newsrooms further exacerbates the issue, leaving an unfilled space that could challenge prevailing narratives.

Central to this systemic bias is the selective framing of stories concerning African Americans. Instances of police violence, for example, are sometimes presented in a manner that perpetuates damaging stereotypes, offering an incomplete narrative of the intricate issues at play. This skewed presentation further entrenches pre-existing prejudices, creating a distorted view of the African American community.

Confronting this deeply ingrained bias necessitates an all-encompassing approach. Studies have shown, and philosophers have admonished, that news organizations must proactively strive to diversify their staff, nurturing an inclusive environment that welcomes a spectrum of perspectives. Moreover, journalists must actively engage with the communities they cover, seeking a profound understanding of the layered issues they report on.

Media literacy stands as a linchpin in combating systemic bias. By equipping audiences with the tools to analyze news coverage critically, individuals become adept at discerning when narratives are skewed or incomplete. That empowerment leads to pursuing diverse sources of information, fostering a more enlightened and nuanced public discourse.

Acknowledging the systemic bias in contemporary news media is not an indictment of individual journalists but rather an acknowledgment of a broader, historical malaise that demands collective redress. By confronting this bias head-on, we take a monumental stride towards a more equitable and just society.

For sure, the pervasive bias against African Americans in today's news media finds its origins in the deeply entrenched wounds of the transatlantic slave trade. Addressing this bias is not only a moral imperative but a crucial step toward a media landscape that authentically mirrors the diversity and richness of our communities. It is a clarion call for us all to work towards a media that stands as a beacon of democracy, providing fair and unbiased representation for all.

It is also a reminder of the ever-lasting importance of the Black Press of America. In 2024, the Black Press of America will observe a remarkable milestone: 197 years of dedication to truth, justice, and equality. Since its inception, which occurred before the end of slavery in America, the Black Press has been a resounding and essential voice, tirelessly advocating for the rights and empowerment of Black communities. As we celebrate this nearly two-century legacy, it's vital to reflect on the profound impact the Black Press has had on the nation and the enduring importance it holds today.

The origins of the Black Press can be traced back to 1827, with the founding of "Freedom's Journal," a pioneering newspaper that laid the foundation for a movement that would shape American history. Samuel Cornish and John Russwurm, the editors of this groundbreaking publication, set out to challenge the oppression and misinformation faced by African Americans during a time of slavery and segregation.

"Freedom's Journal" was not merely a newspaper but a beacon of hope. Its pages highlighted the achievements, struggles, and stories of the Black community, giving a voice to the voiceless and a sense of identity and unity. The newspaper played an instrumental role in the fight for abolition and civil rights, advocating for an end to slavery and establishing equal rights for all.

Throughout its history, the Black Press has chronicled significant moments in the African American journey. From reporting on the Underground Railroad to covering pivotal events like the murder of Emmett Till and the Civil Rights Movement, these publications served as a vital source of information, inspiration, and mobilization for the Black community and its allies. They didn't merely document history; they helped shape it.

The Black Press celebrated Black excellence, from the achievements of scientists, artists, and writers to the emergence of influential leaders who have steered the course of civil rights. It also provided a platform for emerging writers, journalists, and activists, nurturing the next generation and ensuring that the legacy of advocacy journalism persevered.

Today, the Black Press remains an indispensable force in American media. It continues to fill gaps in the coverage of mainstream media, giving voice to marginalized communities and advocating for social justice. These publications, whether in print or online, highlight issues such as racial injustice, economic disparities, and the achievements of Black professionals in various fields.

The Black Press of America has adapted to the digital age, embracing social media, podcasts, and online platforms to reach an even broader audience. This evolution has ensured that its message resonates with new generations, reaffirming its relevance in a changing media landscape.

As we approach the 197th anniversary of the Black Press in 2024 and the bicentennial in 2027, it's crucial to recognize the timeless commitment it represents. In an age where the pursuit of truth, justice, and equality remains a paramount concern, the Black Press continues to serve as a beacon of hope, a platform for expression, and a vehicle for change.

This commitment to advocating for equal rights, giving voice to the marginalized, and chronicling the Black experience is a testament to the enduring significance of the Black Press in shaping American history and its present. It has not only chronicled the struggle but has been an integral part of the struggle itself, making it an indispensable pillar of American journalism.

To be sure, the journey from "Freedom's Journal" to the present day is not only a testament to the past but a beacon of hope for the years to come.

Transatlantic Slave Trade

Overcoming the 500-Year Legacy from 1500 to 2024

*W*hen I was a young civil rights student-worker for the Reverend Dr. Martin Luther King, Jr. and the Southern Christian Leadership Conference (SCLC), I believed in the transformational power of the "Freedom Movement" and the capacity for social-change of the contemporary "Civil Rights Movement" of the 1960s. Golden Frinks, North Carolina State Field Secretary for SCLC, and Milton Fitch, North Carolina State Coordinator for SCLC, recruited me to be the statewide Youth Coordinator for the SCLC when I was fourteen years old in my hometown of Oxford, North Carolina.

Actually, my parents, Benjamin F. Chavis, Sr. and Elisabeth Ridley Chavis, encouraged me to join the Youth Chapter of Granville County Branch of the NAACP when I was 12 years old. Back in those days in the 1950s we all felt it was important to join as many Black organizations as possible, given the omnipresent reality of abject poverty and overt racial discrimination that was systematically consigned and rigidly enforced.

At times we would all ask in our daily prayers for the answers to why our families and communities were targeted for so much racial hatred, violence, prejudice, and economic exploitation. I knew from the first grade in school when I was six years-old and growing up in Oxford, North Carolina, that something was awfully wrong about how "colored people" were being treated in America and Africa and throughout the diaspora. The books that the North Carolina Colored School System mandated for first graders to learn how to read were full of negative, demeaning, and dehumanizing images and stereotypes that depicted African people as embarrassing idiots without any positive attributes or references to our humanity.

One of those books I recall had a demeaning caricature of a young South Indian boy named "Black Sambo." *The Story of Little Black Sambo* written and illustrated by a Scottish author was first published in 1899 in London and led to American versions published with illustrations of Sambo as an African boy. These remained popular until around 1950. Modern versions of the much-criticized controversial editions eventually evolved to changing the racial overtones of the title and the illustrations, including a 2004 Little Golden Books titled *The Boy and the Tigers* with new illustrations and a boy called Little Rajani.*

Fake theology also emerged by some American religious leaders who reattempted to convince us that we were a "cursed people" by the Creator, and therefore the enslavement of African people was considered to have been commanded and ordained by God. The slave masters, the imperial kidnappers, the Atlantic Ocean transporters, the rapists, plantation owners, enslavement insurance providers, and the lynchers were all just doing God's work. Of course, nothing could have been further from the truth. The evil lie of the sinful justification of the global enslavement of African people needed to be exposed and challenged.

I put my age up and got my driver's license also when I was 14 so that I could have the necessary mobility across the state for my work with SCLC. I did not have much time for adolescence. I grew up fast. I was a proud young man with responsibilities. Fighting for freedom was my acknowledged birthright. Being an activist was also uplifting and helped me to be a better student in high school and college.

Frinks was from Edenton, N.C. and Fitch was from Wilson, N.C. Those two towns like Oxford, N.C. were in the eastern North Carolina "Black Belt." That name was derived from the fact that the population in eastern N.C. was predominantly Black, rural and farm centric. Large tobacco, cotton, and rice plantations were still prevalent in that part of the state.

Many of our families could trace our ancestries via the underground oral tradition to one of the regional slave ports in nearby Norfolk, VA,

---

* https://en.wikipedia.org/wiki/The_Story_of_Little_Black_Sambo

Wilmington, N.C., and Charleston, S.C. The brutal enslavement of African people along the eastern coastal regions of the United States for centuries laid the foundation for multiple generations of wealth and financial prominence that still prevail today.

Yet it was during the numerous rallies, marches, and nonviolent civil disobedient demonstrations with SCLC and the NAACP that I witnessed and learned firsthand about the enduring value of keeping belief and faith in the movement's effectiveness even in face of the threats of death, violence, imprisonment, and personal and family hardship. When we frequently would sing one of the anthems of the freedom struggle, "We Shall Overcome," I believed that one day we would eventually overcome. That belief kept us going. That faith kept us speaking out and standing up for freedom, justice, equality, and equity. It was not only aspirational, but it was also exhilarating.

In order to overcome injustice, inequality, inequity, racism, prejudice, hatred, and bigotry, we had to first endeavor to understand better and to admit honestly about why these unprecedented crimes against humanity were sanctioned, embraced, tolerated and violently defended. The true and factual legacy of the Transatlantic Slave Trade is still being denied by nations, governments, institutions and societies unrepentantly for over 500 years.

Now that as I am much older and experienced, I am blessed to have the opportunity and responsibility today to reflect on the historical and present-day impact of the consequential aftermath of the Transatlantic Slave Trade on African people and on all people throughout the world. Crimes against humanity should never be intellectually justified or camouflaged and revised to blame the enslaved for their oppression, victimization, and discrimination.

The following experiences are shared from my life of being involved in the "Freedom Movements" in Africa, the United States, the Caribbean, and in Brazil, as well as the latest research that contributes to my increase in global awareness and knowledge about the enslavement of African people. Yes. I do believe that we shall overcome the legacy of the Transatlantic Slave Trade. But it should not take another 500 years to do so.

Inhumanity begets inhumanity. Deprivation begets deprivation. Genocide unchallenged and not condemned begets more genocide. The denials of what undergirded the centuries long transatlantic slave trade aids and abets the false notion that the truth of those times of human history are without actual documented facts and knowledge. As we review the facts, the truth is indisputable and irrepressible. The iteration and centuries long evolution of the untruthful evil ideology of white supremacy was defined and used to justify the international economic greed and wealth accumulation derived directly from the enslavement, sale, genocide, oppression, and economic exploitation of African people from 1500 to 2024. Yes. The impact of the legacy of the enslavement of African people continues today.

Five hundred twenty-four years is a very long time. Some researchers have concluded that 60 million Africans died during the transatlantic slave trade. No other people on Earth have struggled as long against enslavement and genocide as what African people have suffered and endured for centuries. I caution against any attempt at equivocation or any attempt to quantitatively or qualitatively to compare the genocidal enslavement of African people to other hideous crimes against humanity such as the murderous genocidal oppression of more than six million of Jews during the Holocaust. The genocide and suffering of Jews by Hitler's racist and antisemitic terrorism should never be minimized or forgotten. The Holocaust of the Jewish people has no parallel in human history. And the genocide and enslavement of African people has no parallel in human history.

Racism in all of its forms has to condemned. Antisemitism in all its forms has to be condemned. Crimes against humanity in all forms and manifestations have to be condemned. We all should learn from history to prevent a repeat of the worst tragic atrocities and acts of terrorism in human history.

From the United Nations to the most established academies in the United States and in Europe, if you asked the question "How many African people were murdered or died during the 500 years of the transatlantic slave trade?" you will not get one universally accepted number. Instead, today the numbers range from 12 million to 15 million to 30 million to

60 million. With all the latest technology and research capabilities of nations and acclaimed colleges and universities worldwide, why in 2024 is there still no verified and universally accepted fact-based number with respect to the number of African people who suffered and died during the centuries-long genocide and economic exploitation? Denying the factual quantitative loss of human life during this time is itself a crime against humanity.

I am grateful to the World Future Fund for their updated collective research and presentation of the facts about the global economic trade and enslavement of African people from the 16th to the 19th Century. While some scholars and researchers continue to argue over the facts and statistics about the quantitative impact of transatlantic slave trade, others are beginning to confess to their inadequacy to come to terms with this and to advocate for the truth of what really happened and why the deliberate genocide happened.

According to the World Future Fund, the transatlantic slave trade "was created by white Christian Europeans." Before it was over, as many as 60 million Africans would be killed for the profit of white Christian imperialism. A key reason for the high death toll was the tidal wave of war and desolation that the slave trade unleashed into the heart of Africa. Huge numbers of people died from being marched to the coasts of Africa from the interior and from the endless series of wars produced by the quest for new slaves. Millions more would die in concentration camps at both ends of the sea journey, and significant numbers would die due to the appalling conditions on the slave ships. The financial profits of this slave trade helped build the economic foundations of America. It was not just the south. Northern business interests made huge profits too.*

We consider this specific accounting based on research by the World Future Fund Organization to be the most accurate assessment of the number of Africans who died in the "procurement and enslavement," as well as the transatlantic human trafficking and forced labor of African people during the transatlantic slave trade.

---

* http://www.worldfuturefund.org/Reports/Slavedeathtoll/slaverydeathtoll.html

Sixty million human beings died as a result of that vicious inhumanity for sake of economic profits. Sixty million Africans died!

Keep in mind that enslaved Africans at one point were not even considered to be fully human. They were categorized inhumanely as property and commodities for sale, abuse, breeding, labor, and for economic gain. Categories of race, the economically inspired evolution of the ideology of white supremacy, and racism each had their geneses contemporaneously with the beginning of the enslavement and trade of African people.

As stipulated and documented by the National Museum of African American History and Culture, "Race is a human-invented, shorthand term used to describe and categorize people into various social groups based on characteristics like skin color, physical features, and genetic heredity. Race, while not a valid biological concept, is a real social construction that gives or denies benefits and privileges."*

The term "race" was first defined as a social construct, but in reality it was also an economic illusionary term with no scientific or biological basis or factual evidence of its categorical existence before the 15th century. The phenomenon of race was concocted and fabricated to justify the dehumanization, exploitative oppression, and enslavement of African people.

The National Museum of African American History and Culture again boldly stated this related fact so clearly and well: "American society developed the notion of race early in its formation to justify its new economic system of capitalism, which depended on the institution of forced labor, especially the enslavement of African peoples." Accordingly, the symbiotic connection and relationship between the invented concepts of race, racism, white supremacy, and privilege with the realities of the terrorism and genocidal enslavement of African people have to better understood and affirmed if we are to ever overcome the legacy of the Transatlantic Slave Trade.

The FairPlanet organization's research and editorial team emphasized: "The origin of racism goes back to the colonization of Africa and South America. The enslavement of millions of Africans to exploit the resources of the conquered territories solidified the European's pretension

---

* htpp//nmaahc.si.edu/learn/talking-about-race/topics/historical-foundations-race

of a moral and civilizational superiority of the 'white race'."* Imperialism, colonization, and the evolution of systems and institutions of racism were all established and maintained to satisfy economic greed and expansion of the Western world. FairPlanet further concluded "Racism is conditioned by economic imperatives, but negotiated through culture: religion, literature, art, science and the media."

Andrew Curran writing for *Time Magazine* in 2020 posited : "The histories of slavery and *racism* in the United States have never been more pertinent. This is also the case for the comparatively understudied history of *race* as a concept, without which it is impossible to understand how Europeans and their colonial "descendants" in the United States engineered the most complete and enduring dehumanization of a people in history."†

The reemergence of the Black Lives Matter movement across the U.S. and throughout the world in the wake of the tragic and brutal police murder of George Floyd in Minneapolis, MN, is echoed the fight against the racially motivated and dehumanizing actions toward black people that will continue to reverberate into 2024 and beyond.

Black Lives Matter. African Lives Matter. Of course, we should affirm that all lives matter. We note, however, with an expression of acknowledgment and affirmation to the United Nations for continuing to take steps to reveal, commemorate, and to offer strategies to address and to document present-day impact of the historic global legacy of the Transatlantic Slave Trade. The U.N. has established and funded an international "Outreach Programme on the Transatlantic Slave Trade and Slavery." The U.N. theme on this international matter in 2023 was "Fighting slavery's legacy of racism through transformative education ."‡

We agree with the U.N.'s focus on the need for global transformative public education about the legacy of the enslavement of African people and its 500-year impact today and into the future. There has been so much "miseducation" about the enslavement and trade of African people to use

---

* https://www.fairplanet.org/dossier/racism/the-concept-of-race/

† https ://time.com/5865530/history-race-concept/

‡ https://www.un.org/en/rememberslavery/observance/2023

the words of Dr. Carter G. Woodson in his transformative book entitled *The Mis-Education of the Negro.*

One of the reasons Stacy Brown and I compiled this book was to make another contribution to the anthology of the literature and to support the efforts of many scholars to ensure that the necessary re-education and ongoing education about the transatlantic slave trade for the next 500 years is based on the truth, honesty and the actual facts. The U.N. correctly postulated, "The racist legacy of the Transatlantic Slave Trade reverberates today in harmful prejudices and beliefs which are still being perpetuated and continue to impact people of African descent across the world. Transformative education, which seeks to empower learners to see the social world critically and through an ethical lens to challenge and change the status quo as agents of change, is essential to the work of teaching and learning about slavery in order to end racism and injustice and to build inclusive societies based on dignity and human rights for all people, everywhere."

We agree with the U.N. that education of all of humanity is important to a future world whereby the debilitative and counterproductive legacy of the transatlantic slave trade will be finally and irreversibly overcome. We also affirm that the vast economic derivative gains in the trillions of dollars over the past 500 years as a direct consequence of the hideous international enslavement and trade of African people require proportionate and equitable financial reparations and other forms of economic compensation to generations of African people throughout the African Diaspora.

In December 2013, it is important to note that the U.N. General Assembly adopted the resolution 68/237 that proclaimed 2015–2014 as the International Decade for People of African Descent. The theme of that designated U.N. decade was "People of African descent: recognition, justice and development."*

The U.N. Decade for People of African Descent should conclude with an accurate international accounting of the economic and monetary deriv-

---

* https://www.un.org/en/observances/decade-people-african-descent

ative impact of the enslavement and trade of African people. We affirm the timely importance of the purpose of determining and calculating fair and equitable financial compensation to the generational descendants of the 60 million who died, suffered, and experienced the unprecedented crimes against humanity evidenced during and throughout the past 500 years and aftermath of the transatlantic slave trade. We intend to advocate for the justifiable economic and social relief and ongoing global public education about the enslavement and trade of African people from pre-K through graduate and post-graduate studies.

We, in addition, take considerable note of admiration for the global game-changing academic scholarship and authorship of distinguished African American professor, Dr. Niklole Hannah-Jones, for authoring *The 1619 Project: A New Origin Story.*

Dr. Hannah-Jones's timely and Pulitzer Prize winning anthology continues to be a major step forward in documenting the impact of the transatlantic slave trade, especially in North America. Professor Hannah-Jones brilliantly documented the arrival of the first enslaved Africans who were kidnapped from the West African nation of Angola to arrive in Jamestown, Virginia in 1619. Certainly, Dr. Niklole Hanna-Jones's will continue to help to advance a more fact-based education about the enslavement of African people in America and throughout the African Diaspora.

Overcoming the systematic legacy of injustice, inequality, and economic inequities of the long-termed impact of the Transatlantic Slave Trade also necessitates establishing ongoing outreach and solidarity of concurrent global movements for reparations and other innovative strategies, programs, projects. In addition to working to support tangible, compensatory relief and repairing the damage of the enslavement and trade of African people in the United States, we also have to work to challenge many other nations that have been responsible for the genocide and oppression of African people.

Specifically in the order of the quantitative and magnitude of participating and profiting from the transatlantic slave trade were the following nations: Portugal, Britain (U.K.), Spain, France, the Netherlands, the United States, and Denmark. The collective wealth from all of these nations that was acquired from the 1500s and that continues to be generated today from the enslavement trade of African people amounts to trillions and trillions of U.S. dollars and British pounds.

The nations of Portugal and Britain were the two most involved nations in the early stages of the transatlantic slave trade.*

The National Archives of the government of the United Kingdom currently makes estimates and concludes: "Britain was one of the most successful slave-trading countries. Together with Portugal, the two countries accounted for about 70 percent of all Africans transported to the Americas. Britain was the most dominant between 1640 and 1807 and it is estimated that Britain transported 3.1 million Africans (of whom 2.7 million arrived) to the British colonies in the Caribbean, North and South America and to other countries."

One the largest genocidal concentrations of enslaved and traded Africans was done by the Portuguese forceful kidnapping extractions from the African nation of Angola across the Atlantic to Brazil in South America. Today, 500 years later the Portuguese language is spoken in Angola and in Brazil by millions of people of African descent as a direct result of the colonization and the transatlantic slave trade first led by the nation of Portugal.

The U.K.'s Britannica documented that "By the 1480s Portuguese ships were already transporting Africans for use as slaves on the sugar plantations in the Cape Verde and Madeira islands in the eastern Atlantic." Then Spain and Portugal, it is documented, "Began establishing colonies in the New World about 1500. The Spanish and Portuguese initially enslaved local Indians and put them to work on plantations, but, as the violence of conquest and as European diseases took their toll on the native populations, the Spanish and Portuguese increasingly brought enslaved people over from Africa."†

The good news is there a growing racial justice mobilization and movement challenging existence of environmental racism now rapidly growing

---

* https://www.nationalarchives.gov.uk/help-with-your-research/research-guides/british
-transatlantic-slave-trade-records/

† https://www.britannica.com/summary/Transatlantic-Slave-Trade-Causes-and
-Effects

in Brazil along with the increasing public demands for African and African Brazilian reparations. I was the first person to coin the term "environmental racism" in 1982 in Warren County, North Carolina during racial justice protest against the unjust exposure of Black people to cancer-causing PCBs (Polychlorinated Biphenyls). At Harvard University I recently had the opportunity to meet some the key activists who are protesting and challenging environmental racism in Brazil. They were African Brazilian women leaders and scholars such as Ana Sanches Baptista, Maria Carolina Casati, Amanda Costa, and Izabela Santos.

Without going in further details about the debate over the accurate number of enslaved Africans that were forcibly transported across the Atlantic Ocean to North and South America, the point here is that the magnitude of a problem determines the magnitude of the solution to the problem. Thus, the quantification and determining all of the people, nations, governments, businesses, and institutions who are responsible and all who have been impacted and continue to be impacted as a result of the legacy of the enslavement and trade of African people are important details that should not be overlooked in developing international and national remedies.

In particular, we highlight in solidarity the presence and growing reparations movements related to the ongoing aftermath and socioeconomic legacy of the transatlantic slave trade in North and South America: Jamaica, Trinidad and Tobago, Barbados, Cuba, Grenada, Puerto Rico, Haiti, Dominican Republic, Saint Kitts and Nevis, Bahamas, Bermuda, Dominica, Saint Lucia, Antigua and Barbuda, Saint Vincent and the Grenadines, Belize, Cayman Islands, Turks and Caicos Islands, British Virgin Islands, United States Virgin Islands, United States, Canada, United Kingdom, France, Portugal, Aruba, Anguilla, Curacao, Martinique, Montserrat, Panama, Brazil, Columbia, Argentina, Paraguay, Bolivia, Chile, Uruguay, Ecuador, Peru, Venezuela, Mexico, Costa Rica, Guatemala, Nicaragua, El Salvador, Honduras, and in Suriname.

We are further in solidarity of the issue of reparations with the following African nations that were devastated by the genocide and terrorism of the transatlantic slave trade: Angola, Congo, Democratic Republic of Congo, Ghana, Gabon, Senegal, Gambia, Guinea-Bissau, Mali, Niger, Togo, Benin, Nigeria, Namibia, South Africa, Zambia, Zimbabwe, Botswana, Central African Republic, Uganda, Rwanda, Malawi, Cote D'Ivoire, Guinea, Guinea-Bissau, Sierra Leone, Liberia, Tanzania, Mozambique, Cameroon, Burkina-Faso, and Cape Verde.

Since 2008, the United Nations has declared and observed annually March 25th as the International Day of Remembrance of the Victims of Slavery and the Transatlantic Slave Trade.*

Now it is time to cojoin the international memorial day about the victimization of the enslavement and trade of African people with concrete measures and actions to repair the centuries-long damage.

In conclusion, the statement by A. Missouri Sherman-Peter, United Nations Ambassador and Permanent Observer of the Caribbean Community (CARICOM) forthrightly sums up where we are today in 2024: "It is now universally understood and accepted that the transatlantic trade in enchained, enslaved Africans was the greatest crime against humanity committed in what is now defined as the modern era. In terms of its scale and its social, psychological, spiritual and physical brutality, specifically inflicted upon Africans as a targeted ethnicity, this vastly profitable business, and the considerable subsequent suppression of the inhumanity and criminal nature of slavery, was ubiquitous and usurping of moral values."†

The legacy of 500 years of the transatlantic slave trade each year produces more evidence of the facts and circumstances of that prolonged, international crime against humanity. Yet, each year also provides the responsibility and opportunity to strive to overcome the legacy of the enslavement and trade of African people.

The truth is, as we affirm the oneness of all humanity, all people in every nation impacted by the global enslaved trade should all work together not just to point accusatory fingers at the perpetrators, but also all should work together to ensure that reparations are actually extended to African people who were targeted, enslaved and traded. The generational descendants of enslaved and traded African people should as well

---

* https://www.un.org/en/rememberslavery/observance#:

† https://www.un.org/en/un-chronicle/legacy-slavery-caribbean-and-journey-towards-justice

receive equitable and accountable reparations to initiate an effective and efficient international healing.

There needs to be ongoing affirmative actions by nations, governments, businesses, and institutions to restore and to protect the universal respect of the moral value of all life. The only assurance that the legacy and lingering impact of the Transatlantic Slave Trade will be overcome is to demand, encourage, plan, fund, and to implement the United Nations reparations and restorative justice programs. On September 19, 2023, U.N. Human Rights Chief, Volker Turk emphasized, "It is high time countries made reparatory justice a priority to address the legacy of slavery and colonialism, which continues to negatively impact the daily lives of people of African descent across the globe."

In an official press release issued by the U.N. Office of the High Commissioner for Human Rights the following steps were outlined with respect to the U.N.'s plan for restorative justice .*

> GENEVA /NEW YORK (19 September 2023) – An in-depth UN report focused on reparatory justice for people of African descent, published today, urges States to show strong leadership and political will in tackling the lasting consequences of enslavement, the trade in enslaved Africans and colonialism. The report to the UN General Assembly, by the UN Secretary-General, sets out a series of concrete steps for States and the international community to address the continued harms suffered by people of African descent—highlighting the intrinsic link between the legacies of colonialism and enslavement and contemporary forms of systemic racism and racial discrimination, intolerance and xenophobia faced by people of African descent.

The United Nations report concluded, "that, ultimately, the greatest barrier to reparations for colonialism and enslavement may be that "the biggest beneficiaries of both lack the political will and moral courage to pursue such reparations." We agree with the United Nations that the most

---

* https://www.ohchr.org/en/press-releases/2023/09/strong-leadership-

appropriate and effective measures to overcome the legacy of the transatlantic slave trade with restorative justice and equity include the following:

- ⊙ An official public apology

- ⊙ Global education and awareness

- ⊙ Restitution

- ⊙ Financial Compensation

We would also add the following complimentary and supportive actions:

- ⊙ Academic research and intellectual redress on reparations

- ⊙ International restorative justice and equity media campaign

- ⊙ Sustainable economic development

- ⊙ Inclusive global environmental justice

- ⊙ World Bank and International Monetary Fund loan forgiveness

Yes. I believe that "We Shall Overcome" the legacy of the transatlantic slave trade in Africa, the Caribbean, North America, Central America, South America, Europe and in Asia.

The pendulum of world history is swinging in the direction of equal justice, freedom, equity, and the reaffirmation of the oneness of all humanity. Teaching, learning, and advocating the truth about the enslavement and trade of African people are essential to a more just and equitable world order.

Together in solidarity, spirit, honesty, and in speaking out and standing up to the evils of racism, hatred, injustice, inequity, and dehumanization, "We Shall Overcome."

BENJAMIN F. CHAVIS, JR.
Washington, D.C.

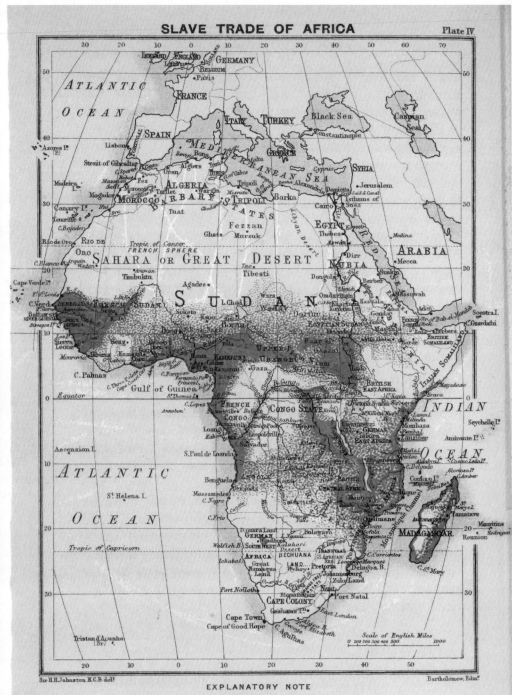

SLAVE TRADE OF AFRICA

Plate IV

An 1899 map of slave trade of Africa

Slave Voyage Tracker

*I*n his PBS series, *Finding Your Roots,* Henry Louis Gates Jr. presents information to guests whose roots cover the globe—from Samoa, Nigeria, Taiwan and Sicily to Iran, Ireland, India and Cuba—and almost everywhere in between.

Each episode weaves together their stories, gleaned from cutting-edge DNA analysis and old school genealogical detective work.

And, at the center of it all and guiding every discovery is Gates, the Alphonse Fletcher University Professor at Harvard University and director of the Hutchins Center for African and African American Research.

Gates is also now featured on a newly updated website, slavevoyages. org, which contains databases of the Trans-Atlantic and Intra-American slave trade.

The databases are the culmination of several decades of independent and collaborative research by scholars who draw upon information in libraries and archives around the world, according to a news release.

The new slave voyages website counts as the product of three years of development by a multi-disciplinary team of historians, librarians, curriculum specialists, cartographers, computer programmers, and web designers, in consultation with scholars of the slave trade from universities in Europe, Africa, South America, and North America.

Among the many unique features are an African names database.

The producers of the site note that during the last 60 years of the transatlantic slave trade, courts around the Atlantic basins condemned over 2,000 vessels for engaging in slave trafficking and recorded the details of captives found on board those ships, including African names.

Links are provided to the ships in the Voyages Database from which the liberated Africans were rescued, as well as to the African Origins site where users can hear the names pronounced and help us identify the languages, they think the names originated from or are used.

The site also takes a deep look at the slave trade within the Americas, which, after the initial disembarkation of African captives in the New World, has received scant attention from historians, especially for the period prior to the abolition of transatlantic slave traffic.

An article on the site examines similar types of intra-American trafficking as an introduction to the launching of the Intra-American Slave Trade Database, which aims to document evidence of slave voyages throughout the New World.

"The site now offers access to details of more than 36,000 slave trading voyages between Africa and the New World; 11,000 voyages from one part of the Americas to another part; and 92,000 Africans who were forced to take the voyage," Gates said.

"Users can analyze data and view videos and they can contribute corrections and add information on voyages the editors don't even know about," he said. The website allows viewers to explore the dispersal of enslaved Africans across the Atlantic world.

According to the website, the digital memorial raises questions about the largest slave trades in history and offers access to the documentation available to answer them.

It recounts how European colonizers turned to Africa for enslaved laborers to build the cities and extract the resources of the Americas. Also, how those colonizers forced millions of mostly unnamed Africans across the Atlantic to the Americas, and from one part of the Americas to another.

Those viewing the website can analyze these slave trades and view interactive maps, timelines, and animations to see the dispersal.

Sponsored by the National Endowment for the Humanities, the work on the site was done at the Emory Center for Digital Scholarship, the University of California at Irvine, and the University of California at Santa Cruz with the Hutchins Center of Harvard University providing support.

"I find it inspiring that our fellow Americans are so determined to explore their own ancestral heritage," Gates noted.

Appendix A

International Decade for People of African Descent, 2015–2024

UN RESOLUTION (68/237)

Resolution adopted by the General Assembly on 23 December 2013 [without reference to a Main Committee (A/68/L.34)] 68/237.

Proclamation of the International Decade for People of African Descent The General Assembly, Recalling its resolution 52/111 of 12 December 1997, by which it decided to convene the World Conference against Racism, Racial Discrimination, Xenophobia and Related Intolerance, and its resolutions 56/266 of 27 March 2002, 57/195 of 18 December 2002, 58/160 of 22 December 2003, 59/177 of 20 December 2004 and 60/144 of 16 December 2005, which guided the comprehensive follow-up to the World Conference and the effective implementation of the Durban Declaration and Programme of Action;

Reiterating that all human beings are born free and equal in dignity and rights and have the potential to contribute constructively to the development and well-being of their societies, and that any doctrine of racial superiority is scientifically false, morally condemnable, socially unjust, and dangerous and must be rejected, together with theories that attempt to determine the existence of separate human races.

Acknowledging the efforts and initiatives undertaken by States to prohibit discrimination and segregation and to engender the full enjoyment of economic, social and cultural as well as civil and political rights.

Emphasizing that, despite efforts in this regard, millions of human beings continue to be victims of racism, racial discrimination, xenophobia and related intolerance, including their contemporary manifestations, some of which take violent forms;

Also emphasizing its resolution 64/169 of 18 December 2009, by which it proclaimed 2011 as the International Year for People of African Descent, Recalling its resolutions 3057 (XXVIII) of 2 November 1973, 38/14 of 22 November 1983, and 48/91 of 20 December 1993, by which it proclaimed the three Decades to Combat Racism and Racial Discrimination, and conscious of the fact that their objectives are yet to be attained, 1. See A/CONF.189/12 and Corr.1, chap. I. A/RES/68/237

Proclamation of the International Decade for People of African Descent 2/2 Underlining its resolution 67/155 of 20 December 2012, by which it requested the President of the General Assembly, in consultation with Member States, relevant United Nations programs and organizations and civil society, including non-governmental organizations, to launch an informal consultative preparatory process for the proclamation of the International Decade for People of African Descent, with the theme "People of African descent: recognition, justice and development", with a view to proclaiming the International Decade in 2013;

Recalling paragraph 61 of its resolution 66/144 of 19 December 2011, by which it encouraged the Working Group of Experts on People of African Descent to develop a program of action, including a theme, for adoption by the Human Rights Council, and in this regard taking note of Council resolution 21/33 of 28 September 2012,2 in which the Council welcomed the draft program of action for the Decade for People of African Descent 3 and decided to transmit it to the General Assembly with a view to its adoption;

Taking note with appreciation of the work undertaken by the Working Group of Experts on People of African Descent in producing a draft program of action that is comprehensive and covers a wide range of areas that could serve as a broad framework for the program of action for the International Decade for People of African Descent, and the report of the Secretary-General on how to make the International Decade effective.

4 1. Proclaims the International Decade for People of African Descent, commencing on:

1. January 2015 and ending on 31 December 2024, with the theme "People of African descent: recognition, justice and development", to be officially launched immediately following the general debate of the sixty-ninth session of the General Assembly.

2. Requests the President of the General Assembly, through the facilitator, to continue consultations with States members of the General Assembly and other stakeholders, with a view to elaborating a program for the implementation of the International Decade, with a draft program developed by the Intergovernmental Working Group on the Effective Implementation of the Durban Declaration and Program of Action as its basis, to be finalized and adopted during the sixty-eighth session of the Assembly and not later than 30 June 2014;

3. Calls for the allocation of predictable funding from the regular budget and extrabudgetary resources of the United Nations for the effective implementation of the program of action and activities under the International Decade.

Appendix B

UN Resolution on Transatlantic Slave Trade

GENERAL ASSEMBLY RESOLUTION 62/122,
ADOPTED DECEMBER 17, 2007

*T*he General Assembly would welcome the erection of the Ark of Return—the permanent memorial to honor the victims of slavery and the transatlantic slave trade—in a prominent place at United Nations Headquarters that would be easily accessible to delegates, staff and visitors, according to a draft resolution it adopted today.

By other terms of the text—which the Assembly adopted without a vote, as it met to commemorate the 200th anniversary of the abolition of slavery and the transatlantic slave trade—the permanent memorial would be erected in acknowledgement of and consideration of the legacy of slavery.

Also, by the text, the Assembly would further express gratitude to the committee of interested States, drawn from all the world's geographical regions, the United Nations Educational, Scientific and Cultural Organization (UNESCO), representatives of the Secretariat and civil society, which had overseen the permanent memorial project.

Further by the text, the Assembly would request the Secretary-General to continue to organize an annual series of activities to commemorate the International Day of Remembrance of the Victims of Slavery and the Transatlantic Slave Trade, including a commemorative meeting of the General Assembly at Headquarters and, as appropriate, activities through the network of United Nations information centers.

By other terms, the Assembly would request that the Secretariat's Department of Public Information, in cooperation with the countries concerned, relevant organizations and entities of the United Nations system, continue to take appropriate steps to enhance world public aware-ness of the commemorative activities and the permanent memorial. The Secretary-General would also be requested to report to the General Assembly at its seventy-third session on continued action to implement a programmed of educational outreach, including actions taken by Member States in implementing the present resolution.

Also, by the text, the United Nations Office for Partnerships, through the Secretary-General, would be requested to submit a comprehensive report to the General Assembly at its seventy-first session on the status of the Trust Fund and, in particular, on contributions received and their utilization. The Assembly would decide to include, in the provisional agenda of its seventy-first session, the item "Commemoration of the aboli-tion of slavery and the transatlantic slave trade."

Mogens Lykketoft (Denmark), President of the General Assem-bly, commended the Department of Public Information in his opening remarks for having selected the theme "Women and slavery" for the 2015 commemoration. Slave women had suffered three-fold, being considered black in a white society, slaves in a free society and women in a society ruled by men, he said, adding that the struggles of millions of descen-dants of enslaved Africans had not ended. The current challenge was to fight all forms of discrimination, including gender discrimination, and to eradicate contemporary forms of slavery, such as sexual slavery, of which women and girls were the primary victims.

Jamaica's representative, presenting the draft resolution "Permanent memorial to and remembrance of the victims of slavery and the transat-lantic slave trade" (document A/70/L.5), said the Caribbean Commu-nity (CARICOM) and African States had collaborated with a wide range of partners to arrive at a text that truly reflected the consensus that the text had enjoyed over the years. Since the Assembly's last consider-ation of the agenda item under discussion, the permanent memorial had been completed and unveiled on 25 March 2015, on time and on budget. However, the work did not cease, she emphasized, pointing out that there remained broad scope for actions to teach present and future generations about the true nature of slavery and how it had been sustained, opposed, and finally defeated.

Sierra Leone's representative, speaking on behalf of the African Group, said that in commemorating the lives lost to slavery and the slave trade, the international community should also celebrate the resilience of the descendants. The tide of slavery had receded, but had not quite gone away, he cautioned, emphasizing that the international community must make sure that a world without slavery truly came about.

Several delegations underscored the need to protect the human rights of the descendants of enslaved Africans, with some calling for reparations to redress the horrific injustices of the past. Colombia's representative noted that the descendants had trodden a long path to claim their rights. The 2015–2024 International Decade for People of African Descent proclaimed by the Assembly in its resolution 68/237 had opened a window for reparations in that regard.

Cuba's representative quoted Fidel Castro's address at the 2001 World Conference against Racism, recalling that the former Cuban President had stated that inhuman exploitation had affected the destiny and lives of more than 4 billion people in the developing world. The descendants of African slaves needed reparations, and developed countries, which had been the beneficiaries of slavery and terrible exploitation, should compensate them.

Several other Latin American delegations highlighted the valuable contributions that descendants of African slaves had made to the cultural and ethnic diversity of their nations.

In other business today, the Assembly concluded its general debate on the revitalization of its work, which had commenced yesterday.

Other speakers today were representatives of India, Israel, United Republic of Tanzania, United States, Kazakhstan, Argentina, Nicaragua, Costa Rica, Tunisia, Morocco, Sudan, San Marino, and Croatia. A representative of the European Union also spoke.

The General Assembly will meet again at 10 a.m. on Thursday, 5 November, to consider the reports of the International Court of Justice and the International Criminal Court.

Appendix C

UN Universal Declaration on Human Rights (1948)

Preamble

Whereas recognition of the inherent dignity and of the equal and inalienable rights of all members of the human family is the foundation of freedom, justice, and peace in the world,

Whereas disregard and contempt for human rights have resulted in barbarous acts which have outraged the conscience of mankind, and the advent of a world in which human beings shall enjoy freedom of speech and belief and freedom from fear and want has been proclaimed as the highest aspiration of the common people,

Whereas it is essential, if man is not to be compelled to have recourse, as a last resort, to rebellion against tyranny and oppression, that human rights should be protected by the rule of law,

Whereas it is essential to promote the development of friendly relations between nations,

Whereas the peoples of the United Nations have in the Charter reaffirmed their faith in fundamental human rights, in the dignity and worth of the human person and in the equal rights of men and women and have determined to promote social progress and better standards of life in larger freedom,

Whereas Member States have pledged themselves to achieve, in co-operation with the United Nations, the promotion of universal respect for and observance of human rights and fundamental freedoms,

Whereas a common understanding of these rights and freedoms is of the greatest importance for the full realization of this pledge,

Now, Therefore THE GENERAL ASSEMBLY proclaims THIS UNIVERSAL DECLARATION OF HUMAN RIGHTS as a common standard of achievement for all peoples and all nations, to the end that every individual and every organ of society, keeping this Declaration constantly in mind, shall strive by teaching and education to promote respect for these rights and freedoms and by progressive measures, national and international, to secure their universal and effective recognition and observance, both among the peoples of Member States themselves and among the peoples of territories under their jurisdiction.

Article 1.

All human beings are born free and equal in dignity and rights. They are endowed with reason and conscience and should act towards one another in a spirit of brotherhood.

Article 2.

Everyone is entitled to all the rights and freedoms set forth in this Declaration, without distinction of any kind, such as race, colour, sex, language, religion, political or other opinion, national or social origin, property, birth, or other status. Furthermore, no distinction shall be made on the basis of the political, jurisdictional or international status of the country or territory to which a person belongs, whether it be independent, trust, non-self-governing or under any other limitation of sovereignty.

Article 3.

Everyone has the right to life, liberty, and security of person.

Article 4.

No one shall be held in slavery or servitude; slavery and the slave trade shall be prohibited in all their forms.

Article 5.

No one shall be subjected to torture or to cruel, inhuman or degrading treatment or punishment.

Article 6.

Everyone has the right to recognition everywhere as a person before the law.

Article 7.

All are equal before the law and are entitled without any discrimination to equal protection of the law. All are entitled to equal protection against any discrimination in violation of this Declaration and against any incitement to such discrimination.

Article 8.

Everyone has the right to an effective remedy by the competent national tribunals for acts violating the fundamental rights granted him by the constitution or by law.

Article 9.

No one shall be subjected to arbitrary arrest, detention or exile.

Article 10.

Everyone is entitled in full equality to a fair and public hearing by an independent and impartial tribunal, in the determination of his rights and obligations and of any criminal charge against him.

Article 11.

(1) Everyone charged with a penal offence has the right to be presumed innocent until proved guilty according to law in a public trial at which he has had all the guarantees necessary for his defense.

(2) No one shall be held guilty of any penal offence on account of any act or omission which did not constitute a penal offence, under national or international law, at the time when it was committed. Nor shall a heavier penalty be imposed than the one that was applicable at the time the penal offence was committed.

Article 12.

No one shall be subjected to arbitrary interference with his privacy, family, home or correspondence, nor to attacks upon his honour and reputation. Everyone has the right to the protection of the law against such interference or attacks.

Article 13.

(1) Everyone has the right to freedom of movement and residence within the borders of each state.

(2) Everyone has the right to leave any country, including his own, and to return to his country.

Article 14.

(1) Everyone has the right to seek and to enjoy in other countries asylum from persecution.

(2) This right may not be invoked in the case of prosecutions genuinely arising from non-political crimes or from acts contrary to the purposes and principles of the United Nations.

Article 15.

(1) Everyone has the right to a nationality.

(2) No one shall be arbitrarily deprived of his nationality nor denied the right to change his nationality.

Article 16.

(1) Men and women of full age, without any limitation due to race, nationality or religion, have the right to marry and to found a family. They are entitled to equal rights as to marriage, during marriage and at its dissolution.

(2) Marriage shall be entered into only with the free and full consent of the intending spouses.

(3) The family is the natural and fundamental group unit of society and is entitled to protection by society and the State.

Article 17.

(1) Everyone has the right to own property alone as well as in association with others.

(2) No one shall be arbitrarily deprived of his property.

Article 18.

Everyone has the right to freedom of thought, conscience and religion; this right includes freedom to change his religion or belief, and freedom, either alone or in community with others and in public or private, to manifest his religion or belief in teaching, practice, worship and observance.

Article 19.

Everyone has the right to freedom of opinion and expression; this right includes freedom to hold opinions without interference and to seek, receive and impart information and ideas through any media and regardless of frontiers.

Article 20.

(1) Everyone has the right to freedom of peaceful assembly and association.

(2) No one may be compelled to belong to an association.

Article 21.

(1) Everyone has the right to take part in the government of his country, directly or through freely chosen representatives.

(2) Everyone has the right of equal access to public service in his country.

(3) The will of the people shall be the basis of the authority of government; this will shall be expressed in periodic and genuine elections which shall be by universal and equal suffrage and shall be held by secret vote or by equivalent free voting procedures.

Article 22.

Everyone, as a member of society, has the right to social security and is entitled to realization, through national effort and international co-operation and in accordance with the organization and resources of each State, of the economic, social, and cultural rights indispensable for his dignity and the free development of his personality.

Article 23.

(1) Everyone has the right to work, to free choice of employment, to just and favourable conditions of work and to protection against unemployment.

(2) Everyone, without any discrimination, has the right to equal pay for equal work.

(3) Everyone who works has the right to just and favourable remuneration ensuring for himself and his family an existence worthy of human dignity, and supplemented, if necessary, by other means of social protection.

(4) Everyone has the right to form and to join trade unions for the protection of his interests.

Article 24.

Everyone has the right to rest and leisure, including reasonable limitation of working hours and periodic holidays with pay.

Article 25.

(1) Everyone has the right to a standard of living adequate for the health and well-being of himself and of his family, including food, clothing, housing and medical care and necessary social services, and the right to security in the event of unemployment, sickness, disability, widowhood, old age or other lack of livelihood in circumstances beyond his control.

(2) Motherhood and childhood are entitled to special care and assistance. All children, whether born in or out of wedlock, shall enjoy the same social protection.

Article 26.

(1) Everyone has the right to education. Education shall be free, at least in the elementary and fundamental stages. Elementary education shall be compulsory. Technical and professional education shall be made generally available and higher education shall be equally accessible to all on the basis of merit.

(2) Education shall be directed to the full development of the human personality and to the strengthening of respect for human rights and fundamental freedoms. It shall promote understanding, tolerance, and friendship among all nations, racial or religious groups, and shall further the activities of the United Nations for the maintenance of peace.

(3) Parents have a prior right to choose the kind of education that shall be given to their children.

Article 27.

(1) Everyone has the right freely to participate in the cultural life of the community, to enjoy the arts and to share in scientific advancement and its benefits.

(2) Everyone has the right to the protection of the moral and material interests resulting from any scientific, literary, or artistic production of which he is the author.

Article 28.

Everyone is entitled to a social and international order in which the rights and freedoms set forth in this Declaration can be fully realized.

Article 29.

(1) Everyone has duties to the community in which alone the free and full development of his personality is possible.

(2) In the exercise of his rights and freedoms, everyone shall be subject only to such limitations as are determined by law solely for the purpose of securing due recognition and respect for the rights and freedoms of others and of meeting the just requirements of morality, public order and the general welfare in a democratic society.

(3) These rights and freedoms may in no case be exercised contrary to the purposes and principles of the United Nations.

Article 30.

Nothing in this Declaration may be interpreted as implying for any State, group or person any right to engage in any activity or to perform any act aimed at the destruction of any of the rights and freedoms set forth herein.

Appendix D

Strong Leadership and Political will crucial to ensure reparatory justice for people of African descent—UN Report

19 September 2023

GENEVA/NEW YORK (19 September 2023) – An in-depth UN report, focused on reparatory justice for people of African descent, published today, urges States to show strong leadership and political will in tackling the lasting consequences of enslavement, the trade in enslaved Africans and colonialism.

The report to the UN General Assembly, by the UN Secretary-General, sets out a series of concrete steps for States and the international community to address the continued harms suffered by people of African descent—highlighting the intrinsic link between the legacies of colonialism and enslavement and contemporary forms of systemic racism and racial discrimination, intolerance, and xenophobia faced by people of African descent.

"It is estimated that between 25 and 30 million people were violently uprooted from Africa for enslavement. The transatlantic trade in enslaved Africans caused the largest and most concentrated deportation of human beings involving several regions of the world during more than four centuries," the report states.

"Slavery and the slave trade are prohibited under international human rights law, and enslavement has been recognized among the acts constituting, under specific circumstances, a crime against humanity."

The report stresses that the formal abolition of enslavement, and decolonization processes, did not dismantle racially discriminatory structures. Instead, they "gave way to racially discriminatory policies and systems, including segregation and apartheid, that perpetuated racial discrimination, oppression, and inequalities."

For decades, people of African descent across the globe have called for accountability and redress for harms. The report highlights that these demands—including the right to adequate, effective, prompt and appropriate remedies, and reparation for victims of violations of human rights —are enshrined in international and regional human rights instruments.

Although some States have recently taken steps towards addressing past legacies, the report emphasizes that "no State has comprehensively accounted for the past and addressed its contemporary legacies and ongoing manifestations."

The report provides an overview of a variety of measures that can contribute to achieving reparatory justice—with processes "tailored to the specificities of the situation in the country and to the demands of affected communities."

While there is no one-size-fits-all model of reparatory justice, what is clear is that efforts must be guided by people of African descent, particularly women and youth, through their effective and meaningful participation, it states.

Those measures include truth-seeking and truth-telling processes, public apology and acknowledgment, memorialization, education and awareness raising, restitution, medical and psychological rehabilitation, compensation, as well as guarantees of non-repetition.

While assessment of economic damage can be complex owing to the length of time that has passed and the difficulty of identifying perpetrators and victims, "such difficulties cannot be the basis for nullifying the existence of underlying legal obligations."

The report concludes that, ultimately, the greatest barrier to reparations for colonialism and enslavement may be that "the biggest beneficiaries of both lack the political will and moral courage to pursue such reparations."

UN High Commissioner for Human Rights Volker Türk said it was paramount that "strong leadership and political will from States and the international community be galvanized to finally, comprehensively address the entrenched legacies of colonialism, enslavement and the trade in enslaved Africans."

"Reparatory justice is not just about addressing the wrongful acts of the past; it is about building societies that are truly inclusive, equal and free from racism and racial discrimination. A comprehensive approach should, therefore, address the past, present, and future," Türk said.

The report cites examples of States and regional bodies that have acknowledged the need for reparatory justice for people of African descent, such as the CARICOM, the European Parliament and the African Commission on Human and Peoples' Rights. The report also encourages States to actively engage in the elaboration of a draft UN declaration on the promotion and full respect of the human rights of people of African descent, which could provide a global framework to address the systemic nature of racism and racial discrimination.

It adds that private actors, including business enterprises, the media, and educational institutions, should also consider their own links to enslavement and colonialism in their ongoing and past operations and examine possibilities for reparations.

"It is high time reparatory justice is made a priority, to address one of the biggest injustices in human history, and one that continues to negatively impact the daily lives of people of African descent across the globe," Türk stressed.

The report builds upon contributions and recommendations made by United Nations bodies and the High Commissioner's reports over decades, and is a follow-up to the adoption on July 27, 2021, of Resolution HRC 47, The Human Rights Council and Agenda Towards Transformative Change for Racial Justice and Equality.

Epilogue

African Union Ambassador Dr. Arikana Chihombori-Quao's Address to the NNPA at its Midwinter Training Conference in Florida, January 2019

THE WAKANDA ONE VILLAGE PROJECT

*D*r. Arikana Chihombori-Quao, a distinguished figure in African diplomacy, has emerged as a prominent advocate for Pan-African unity and empowerment. As the African Union Ambassador to the United States from 2017 to 2019, Dr. Chihombori-Quao left an indelible mark with her passionate advocacy for African heritage, culture, and socio-economic progress.

Born in Zimbabwe, Dr. Chihombori-Quao's journey to becoming a leading voice in African diplomacy began with a solid educational foundation. She holds a Doctor of Medicine degree, earned in the United States, and has subsequently specialized in family medicine. Her medical career spanned over three decades, contributing to healthcare and public health initiatives.

Dr. Chihombori-Quao's tenure as the African Union Ambassador to the United States was notable for her fervent dedication to promoting the interests of the African diaspora and fostering closer ties between Africa and its international partners. Her advocacy extended to economic empowerment, education, and cultural exchange, focusing on strengthening the bonds between Africa and its diasporic communities.

One of Dr. Chihombori-Quao's key initiatives was the promotion of economic empowerment for people of African descent. She emphasized the potential of a united African diaspora to contribute to the socio-economic development of both the African continent and its global communities.

Dr. Chihombori-Quao was a staunch advocate for preserving and celebrating African heritage and culture. She emphasized the importance of recognizing Africa's rich and diverse history while dispelling stereotypes and misconceptions that have hindered the continent's progress.

During her term as African Union Ambassador, Dr. Chihombori-Quao's advocacy garnered attention and admiration on the global stage. Her impassioned speeches, tireless efforts, and commitment to African unity resonated with audiences worldwide.

Since her tenure as Ambassador, Dr. Chihombori-Quao has remained influential in Pan-African circles. Her work continues through various initiatives to foster dialogue, cooperation, and empowerment within the African diaspora.

Dr. Chihombori-Quao's tenure as the African Union Ambassador to the United States is a testament to her unwavering dedication to Pan-Africanism. Her advocacy for cultural awareness, economic empowerment, and closer ties between Africa and its global diaspora has left a lasting impact on the trajectory of African diplomacy. Dr. Chihombori-Quao's legacy inspires future generations of African leaders and advocates, illustrating the transformative power of unity, cultural pride, and economic empowerment in pursuing a stronger, more connected Africa.

As she entered her office in Northwest Washington, D.C., African Union (AU) Ambassador to the United States, Dr. Arikana Chihombori-Quao, struck observers as an image of grace. With the colors of her beloved Africa draped around her neck, her purple dress perfectly exuded royalty—though likely not intended.

The ambassador's words are unchoreographed, seasoned with salt and a charm that clearly communicates that she should never be thought of as someone whose opinions are easily swayed.

Far from it.

Dr. Chihombori-Quao knows that the world has long mistreated and neglected Africans —particularly the African woman. "We are the original people, and we have every reason to stand up in the tallest mountains to proclaim who we are," the ambassador says unapologetically.

"We are beautiful, intelligent, sophisticated, highly adaptable and totally indestructible people—the Africans," she said. "Any other race that would have gone through what we've been subjected to would have been extinct and that's the truth," she said, never having to raise her voice because the conviction in which she speaks is loud and unmistakably clear.

"Also, as black women, we are the only ones who could reproduce ourselves," the Ambassador said in a room that contained a few men and just one other woman.

The men in the room, which included this reporter, could only agree.

"We could mate with anyone and produce a black child," she said.

"Normally, that's what you see with dominant species. It's a fact they may not like to hear, but ours is the dominate gene. That's why I say when I speak people may get offended, but I come from a place of truth and fact."

The place that Dr. Chihombori-Quao "comes from" has many in the diaspora excited about the future—a future that could finally see Africa return to its former glory.

Married to the highly respected physician Dr. Nii Saban Quao, Dr. Arikana Chihombori-Quao grew up in a small village in Chivhu, Zimbabwe.

She completed her undergraduate education at Fisk University in Nashville, Tenn., and later matriculated at Meharry Medical College where she earned degrees in general chemistry, a master's degree in organic chemistry and a Doctor of Medicine.

After practicing medicine for 25 years, she's actively been involved in numerous AU programs and projects and served as chair of the African Union-Diaspora Health Initiative, where she helped mobilize health professionals in the diaspora to assist in addressing the health care needs of the African continent.

Since accepting the AU Ambassador position, Her Excellency has earned praise as a leader whose brought renewed energy and new ideas to the AU Mission.

A Fellow of the American Academy of Family Physicians, H.E. Dr. Chihombori-Quao also received an achievement award from the late civil rights champion Nelson Mandela.

"How do you transition from being a medical doctor to a diplomat? It took me about six months to finally process it and eventually say, well maybe this is something I can do," she said.

"It's a man's world and I didn't know if I could deal with that, but after much back and forth, I had a conversation with the chair of the African Union, and she told me that she felt a medical doctor would make a good diplomat."

The former Chairperson of the African Union Commission for the continent, H.E. Dr. Nkosazana Dlamini Zuma, is also a medical doctor.

H.E. Dr. Chihombori-Quao continued:

"It might surprise you that quite often patients come to you and need help, but they may not be truthful. They may say they have a headache, but the real problem is an abusive husband. A belly ache might be . . . mental.

"You try to reach out and find out what's going on at home and in their life. I can honestly say I find myself in many situations where being an experienced doctor comes through in this job."

Still, among the defining circumstances that led to Her Excellency accepting the Ambassador's position is her love of Africa and her desire to turn things around on the continent. "It became increasingly apparent how we feel as Africans doesn't matter. We are disrespected and we really needed a voice," she said.

"That's what this mission is all about—being a voice for all Africans on the continent. Once I realized that, I decided I would stay on the job. I needed to be here."

Surprisingly, the Ambassador said she's received virtually no push back. "It's easy for us as our point of view as Africans is that we are in the right. We are coming from the point of righteousness. There's no other way to slice it; it is what it is," she said.

H.E. Dr. Chihombori-Quao is among those leading the push to undo what occurred at the Berlin Conference 134 years ago when the various European powers salaciously explored, divided, conquered, and exploited the entire African continent.

Known as "The Scramble for Africa," thirteen European countries and the United States met in Berlin and made rules that divided Africa in 53 separate nations.

"They were haphazardly going into Africa to grab whatever they could ... [they said] let's organize so we could effectively loot them," H.E. Dr. Chihombori-Quao said. "That strategy is still in place, unabated with nobody challenging it. It's just accepted," she said.

Her Excellency said Africans must stop accepting crumbs off the table and get a seat at the top of the table itself.

Although it's estimated that $50 billion leaves Africa each year because of corruption, Dr. Chihombori-Quao notes that France still extracts a colonial tax of $500 billion annually from francophone African countries.

"If we talk corruption, we need to talk about it from A to Z. Let's talk about all of this," she said. "The former colonizers are still very active in Africa. You can look at Britain, France, Spain, Belgium, Germany... they are still very present in Africa, yet we don't talk about it."

However, if this Ambassador has her way—and there's little doubt that she can succeed —things will change.

A major part of that change is a new "Wakanda" project launched by Her Excellency that's expected to raise $5 billion in development funding over the next year or so. "The Wakanda One Village Project," will be funded by Africans throughout the diaspora who will be its sole owners.

It will consist of five African Centers of Excellence in each of the five regions of the continent, which will serve as nerve centers for development delivering state-of-the-art healthcare facilities, hotels, industrial homes, shopping centers and other amenities.

"We are going to build the Africa that we want so those [throughout the diaspora] who say I cannot go home because home is not what I am used to will make it what they want," Dr. Chihombori-Quao said.

About the National Newspaper Publishers Association

The National Newspaper Publishers Association—NNPA—is a trade association of the more than 200 African American-owned community newspapers from around the United States.

Since its founding more than 80 years ago, NNPA has consistently been the voice of the black community.

The Black Press believes that America can best lead the world away from racial and national antagonisms when it accords to every person, regardless of race, color or creed, full human, and legal rights.

Hating no person, the Black Press strives to help every person in the firm belief that all are hurt as long as anyone is held back.

About the Black Press of America

In the corridors of American journalism, few entities have stood the test of time and fervently championed the cause of justice and equality like the Black Press. Originating in the crucible of racial discord, this powerful force has evolved over the years, continually reshaping its mission to meet the demands of a changing society.

The Black Press emerged at a critical juncture in American history when the shackles of slavery had yet to be broken, and a new era of promise and turmoil was about to begin. *Samuel Cornish and John B. Russwurm established Freedom's Journal in 1827 as a clarion call for African Americans to assert their rights and share their experiences. Cornish and Russwurm boldly declared on the front pages, "We wish to plead our own cause; for too long, others have spoken for us."* This groundbreaking publication paved the way for a wave of Black-owned newspapers, each committed to providing a platform for marginalized voices.

As the 19th century marched forward, luminaries like Ida B. Wells-Barnett, who fearlessly documented the horrors of lynching in her newspaper, *The Memphis Free Speech*, and T. Thomas Fortune, a staunch advocate for civil rights through his paper, *The New York Age*, added new dimensions to the Black Press. They were trailblazers, challenging the status quo and shaping a narrative that would ultimately redefine American society.

The mid-20th century was an epochal period for the Black Press. With the Civil Rights Movement in full swing, newspapers like *The Chicago Defender* and *The Pittsburgh Courier* were at the forefront of change. They not only reported on the pivotal events and leaders of the era but also served as mobilization tools, galvanizing communities across the nation.

In the hallowed pages of these publications, the stories of Rosa Parks, Fannie Lou Hamer, and the indomitable Martin Luther King Jr. were etched indelibly, immortalizing their struggles and triumphs. The Black Press was the voice of the disenfranchised, a megaphone for those demanding their rightful place in the American tapestry.

In the present day, the Black Press remains as relevant and crucial as ever. The National Newspaper Publishers Association (NNPA) is a steadfast advocate for the over 240 Black-owned newspapers that continue to provide a vital voice to their communities. These publications, from *The Washington Informer* and Baltimore AFRO to *The St. Louis American* to the *Los Angeles Sentinel* and the *Omaha Star*, bridge the gaps in information access and highlight the multifaceted experiences of African Americans.

The core tenet of the Black Press is an unwavering belief in the intrinsic value of every human being, regardless of their background. This belief is more than rhetoric; it is a guiding principle that informs every story, every editorial decision, and every call to action. It's a conviction that has been forged in the crucible of adversity and tested through the annals of history.

In a world still grappling with divisions, the Black Press holds steadfast to a vision where America leads the way in dismantling racial and national hatred. They reject hate and discrimination, embracing the belief that progress for one is progress for all. It's a vision of unity, where the advancement of each individual propels the collective journey toward justice and equality.

As we reflect on the legacy of the Black Press, we are reminded that their story is not just a chapter in American history but a testament to the enduring power of journalism to shape societies and uplift humanity. Their journey is a beacon of hope, a reminder that the fight for justice is a continuum and that every voice and every story is a force for change. The Black Press stands tall, reminding us that the arc of history may be long, but it inevitably bends toward justice.

Index

About Dr. Benjamin F. Chavis, Jr.

Benjamin F. Chavis, Jr. a global business leader, educator, and longtime civil rights activist, was elected president and CEO of the National Newspaper Publishers Association at the group's annual meeting in 2014.

Chavis is president of Education Online Services Corporation (EOServe Corp.), the premier provider of online higher education for Historically Black Colleges and Universities (HBCUs).

He is also president, CEO and Co-Founder with Russell Simmons of the Hip-Hop Summit Action Network (HSAN), the world's largest coalition of hip-hop artists and recording industry executives and a community of leaders dedicated to fighting poverty and injustice.

Chavis has served on numerous boards, including the National Association for Equal Opportunity in Higher Education (NAFEO).

He was the leader of the Wilmington Ten, a group of wrongly convicted activists who were recently pardoned by North Carolina Gov. Bev Perdue; a former president of the NAACP (1993–1994) and in 1995 served as director and chief organizer of the Million Man March.

Chavis writes a weekly syndicated column for the NNPA News Service. "Dr. Chavis has the talent, contacts and energy to make an immediate impact on our organization, which represents approximately 200 African American newspapers in the U.S," said Arizona Informant Publisher Cloves Campbell, who once served as NNPA chairman.

Upon his election as president and CEO, Chavis said, "I am honored to have the opportunity to serve, promote and secure the interests of the National Newspaper Publishers Association (NNPA). As the uncensored, objective, unflinching media voice of Black America, NNPA newspapers, the NNPA News Service and the companion site, BlackPressUSA.com, represent one of the most important newsgathering and news analysis operations in the world."

Chavis continued, "I am eager to deliver trusted, sustainable, and innovative relationships for the NNPA with advertisers, partners, sponsors, and supporters. More than ever before, the leadership and readership of NNPA newspapers and BlackPressUSA are important to the future of America and the global community."

A native of Oxford, North Carolina, Chavis received his Bachelor of Arts in chemistry from the University of North Carolina; his Master of Divinity from Duke University (magna cum laude) and a Doctor of Ministry from Howard University.

An ordained minister in the United Church of Christ, Dr. Chavis began his career in 1963 as a North Carolina statewide youth coordinator for Dr. Martin Luther King, Jr., and the Southern Christian Leadership Conference (SCLC). In 1970, Chavis was appointed Southern Regional Program Director of the 1.7 million-member United Church of Christ Commission for Racial Justice (UCC-CRJ) and in 1985 was named Executive Director and CEO of the UCC-CRJ. In 1988, Dr. Chavis was elected Vice President of the National Council of Churches of the USA.

Chavis has worked extensively in Africa and the Caribbean. He is a senior adviser and former president of the Diamond Empowerment Fund, which supports higher education scholarships in Africa.

About Stacy M. Brown

Stacy M. Brown is a veteran journalist and author of the new biography: *Celebrity Trials: Legacies Lost, Lives Shattered: So What's the Real Truth?*

He's also the coauthor of *Blind Faith: The Miraculous Journey of Lula Hardaway, Stevie Wonder's Mother* and the author of *Michael Jackson: The Man Behind the Mask* and *Fighting Temptation: The Damon Harris Story.*

Stacy has appeared on *Today, NBC Nightly News, Good Morning America, CNN with Don Lemon, Anderson Cooper, Wendy Williams, Howard Stern,* and other shows. He has worked for the past ten years at the NNPA, where he serves as the senior national correspondent covering politics, breaking news, community news, sports, and hosts the NNPA's flagship live show, "Let It Be Known."